Lecture Notes in Computer Science 752

Edited by G. Goos and J. Hartmanis

Advisory Board: W. Brauer D. Gries J. Stoer

Timothy W. Finin   Charles K. Nicholas
Yelena Yesha (Eds.)

Information and Knowledge Management

Expanding the Definition
of "Database"

First International Conference, CIKM '92
Baltimore, Maryland, USA
November 8-11, 1992
Select Papers

Springer-Verlag

Berlin Heidelberg New York
London Paris Tokyo
Hong Kong Barcelona
Budapest

Series Editors

Gerhard Goos
Universität Karlsruhe
Postfach 69 80
Vincenz-Priessnitz-Straße 1
D-76131 Karlsruhe, Germany

Juris Hartmanis
Cornell University
Department of Computer Science
4130 Upson Hall
Ithaca, NY 14853, USA

Volume Editors

Timothy W. Finin
Charles K. Nicholas
Yelena Yesha
University of Maryland Baltimore County, Computer Science Department
5401 Wilkens Avenue, Baltimore, MD 21228-5398, USA

CR Subject Classification (1991): H.2.3-4, H.3.4, H.2.1, I.2.7

ISBN 3-540-57419-0 Springer-Verlag Berlin Heidelberg New York
ISBN 0-387-57419-0 Springer-Verlag New York Berlin Heidelberg

Typesetting: Camera-ready by author
Printing and binding: Druckhaus Beltz, Hemsbach/Bergstr.
45/3140-543210 - Printed on acid-free paper

Preface

The First International Conference on Information and Knowledge Management was held in Baltimore November 8–11, 1992. Over 200 participants from twenty-one countries attended. A major theme of the conference was the degree to which the fields of database, artificial intelligence, and information retrieval overlap and enrich each other.

For this volume, the editors solicited expanded and updated versions of some of the best papers presented at CIKM'92. The scope of the term "database" has broadened considerably over the last several years, to include types of data, and means of organizing that data, that were unknown even ten years ago. Each paper included in this volume illustrates this point.

- In his paper "Discovering Context in a Conceptual Schema", Semmel shows how the knowledge embedded in the conceptual schema of a database can be used to generate queries. In his QUICK system, the conceptual schema is mined for contextual information which is then used to help the user formulate complicated SQL queries. The extraction of conceptual information can also expose subtle flaws in the database design.
- In their paper "An Interactive Image Management System for Face Information Retrieval", Bach, Paul, and Jain describe their *Xenomania* system. They base their design on a general architecture for visual information management systems that provides for the query and retrieval features of ordinary databases, and image understanding techniques. *Xenomania* also uses domain knowledge about human faces, and relevance feedback, to assist and guide users during the search process.
- In their paper "Queries in Object–Oriented Database Systems", Alhajj and Arkun present an algebra and query language for object-oriented databases. Operations in the algebra and query language are characterized in terms a set of objects and a set of message expressions understood by those objects. The algebra satisfies the closure property, which means that the results of operations are objects in the algebra in their own right. This approach therefore allows for the creation of new objects, as well as the manipulation of existing objects in the algebra.
- In their paper "Consistency Checking in Object Oriented Databases: a Behavioral Approach", Martin, Adiba, and Defude show how database consistency and integrity constraints can be associated with the operations defined in an object-oriented database system. Their system provides for the definition of local constraints, which are applied to operations within a transaction, and global constraints, which apply to the transaction as a whole.
- In their paper "Integrity Constraints Representation in Object–Oriented Databases", Formica and Missikoff present TQL, a data definition language for object–oriented databases. TQL provides for the specification of integrity constraints within the database schema, where they can be checked statically

(when the database is first created) or at runtime. The syntax and semantics of TQL are described in detail.

- In their paper "A Framework for Temporal Object Databases", Pissinou and Makki describe T-3DIS, an object database model with extensions to support temporal data, including the semantics of time and the temporal evolution of data. T-3DIS allows for the definition, description, and classification of temporal data objects, and provides a set of operations for manipulating these temporal objects.

- In their paper "Inductive Dependencies and Approximate Databases", Keen and Rajasekar describe a way of generating approximate results to a query for which the information needed for an exact result is missing. The approximations are generated by inductive dependencies, which have a heuristic character that makes them more flexible, if less precise, than functional dependencies. Guard conditions may be associated with an inductive dependency, giving the designer more control over how the approximations are generated.

- In their paper "Object–Oriented Database Design Methodologies: A Survey", Song and Park present a comprehensive overview of tools and techniques for the design of object–oriented database schemata.

Timothy Finin
Charles Nicholas
Yelena Yesha

Baltimore, Maryland
August 1993

Table of Contents

Discovering Context in a Conceptual Schema   1
Ralph. D. Semmel

An Interactive Image Management System
for Face Information Retrieval   16
Jeffrey R. Bach, Santanu Paul, and Ramesh Jain

Queries in Object–Oriented Database Systems   36
Reda Alhajj and M. Erol Arkun

Consistency Checking in Object–Oriented Databases:
A Behavioral Approach   53
Herve Martin, Michel Adiba, and Bruno Defude

Integrity Constraints Representation
in Object–Oriented Databases   69
Anna Formica and Michele Missikoff

A Framework for Temporal Object Databases   86
Niki Pissinou and Kia Makki

Inductive Dependencies and Approximate Databases   98
Debby Keen and Arcot Rajasekar

Object–Oriented Database Design Methodologies:
A Survey   115
Il-Yeol Song and E. K. Park

Discovering Context in a Conceptual Schema

R. D. Semmel

The Johns Hopkins University Applied Physics Laboratory
Laurel, MD 20723
rds@aplcen.apl.jhu.edu

Abstract. While significant effort is expended in developing a conceptual model for an information system, critical knowledge is discarded during implementation. Consequently, designers and users must employ less complete logical level knowledge to access data. Unfortunately, many users do not possess the detailed logical level knowledge required to formulate queries corresponding to ad hoc requests. By using the conceptual schema directly, however, it is possible to formulate such queries automatically. This paper describes how to augment the conceptual schema with knowledge of strongly associated conceptual level objects so that automated query formulation, semantic query optimization, and design feedback are supported. As a result, the conceptual schema assumes a central role throughout an information system's life cycle, and the design of intelligent interfaces is facilitated.

1   Introduction

In the information systems life cycle, significant effort is expended in requirements collection, analysis, and design. In particular, the design of a system's database must facilitate straightforward and efficient data access. To assist with database creation, conceptual design methodologies have been developed that support intuitive approaches for representing an application domain. However, the resulting conceptual schema typically is not used beyond the conceptual modeling phase. Rather, the conceptual schema is mapped to an implementation-dependent logical schema, which is less intuitive and sparser in its representation of essential domain knowledge. All manipulation of the database, including ad hoc querying, must employ this sparser logical schema.

In this paper, a way to reduce the semantic gap that exists between the conceptual and logical schemas is discussed. Specifically, a means of inferring user context is described that enables ad hoc access to be achieved via the conceptual schema. Consequently, the conceptual schema remains an integral component of an information system throughout the system's life cycle. In addition, the paper highlights how the conceptual schema can serve as the basis for semantic query optimization and design feedback.

In the next section, conceptual database design is reviewed, with emphasis on the knowledge available in an extended Entity-Relationship model. Then, it is shown how a conceptual schema can be employed to infer likely user intent. In the fourth section, an example is presented to demonstrate how conceptual schema and context knowledge can be used for query formulation and semantic query optimization. Next, a prototype system that implements the ideas presented is discussed, and a methodology for design feedback is described. Finally, some future research is outlined.

2 Conceptual Database Design

During the past two decades considerable research has been conducted in the development of semantic data models that facilitate schema design. In particular, a high-level conceptual schema first is designed using a semantic data model and then translated into a traditional (e.g., relational, network, or hierarchical) model for implementation [5]. Semantic data models attempt to capture the rich semantics inherent in a complex system. As a result of the intuitive representation supported by these models, communication is facilitated between software designers and users. Consequently, users can play a more integral role in design than would be possible if only logical schema constructs (e.g., relations and dependencies) were used.

While a large number of semantic data models have been proposed, the most popular is the Entity-Relationship (ER) model. Developed by Chen [2], the model has been extended by researchers to facilitate representation of more complex abstractions. Figure 1 illustrates a basic ER diagram for a simple banking example. This example is popular in the universal relation literature, where all attributes are viewed as belonging to a single, universal relation, regardless of the logical database design [10, 11, 19]. As will be described in the next two sections, the ER model provides a natural mechanism for realizing universal relation interfaces.

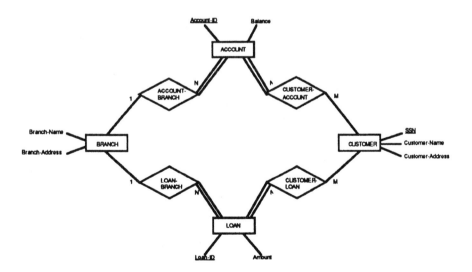

Fig. 1. Banking example conceptual schema.

As illustrated in Figure 1, entity types are represented by rectangles and relationship types are represented by diamonds. In addition, the diagram represents various structural constraints using the notation of Elmasri and Navathe [3]. In particular, edges are labeled with cardinality ratio constraints. For example, CUSTOMER-ACCOUNT is a many-to-many relationship type as customers can have many accounts and accounts can be jointly owned. Similarly, a double-line edge indicates that each entity in an entity set must participate in a relationship, whereas a single-line edge indicates optional participation. Thus, every account must be owned by at least one customer, but not every customer must own accounts. Mapping to the logical level, the diagram can be represented by the following set of relation schemas:

```
BRANCH (BRANCH-NAME, BRANCH-ADDRESS)
CUSTOMER (SSN, CUSTOMER-NAME, CUSTOMER-ADDRESS)
ACCOUNT (ACCOUNT-ID, BALANCE, BRANCH-NAME)
LOAN (LOAN-ID, AMOUNT, BRANCH-NAME)
CUSTOMER-ACCOUNT (SSN, ACCOUNT-ID)
CUSTOMER-LOAN (SSN, LOAN-ID)
```

As described, the ER model can be used to represent simple application domains. Complex domains, however, require more sophisticated representation constructs. Consequently, extensions to the ER model have been proposed that draw upon abstractions commonly used in network knowledge representation schemes (e.g., frames and semantic networks) [12]. In particular, the abstractions of aggregation and generalization proposed by Smith and Smith [16] have been incorporated in several extended ER models [1, 17].

Figure 2 shows a generalization hierarchy, again using the notation of Elmasri and Navathe [3]. In the figure, circles denote both the type of generalization and the association between parents and children. Thus, PERSON is an entity type that has two overlapping subclasses of FACULTY and STUDENT. Similarly, STUDENT has two disjoint subclasses. Moreover, every student must be either a graduate student or an undergraduate student (as indicated by the mandatory participation double-line edge), whereas each person need not necessarily be a faculty member or a student.

At the logical level, the inheritance hierarchy shown in Figure 2 could be represented by the following set of relation schemas:

```
PERSON (SSN, NAME, ADDRESS)
FACULTY (SSN, RANK)
STUDENT (SSN, STATUS)
GRADUATE-STUDENT (SSN, PROGRAM)
UNDERGRAD-STUDENT (SSN, CLASS)
```

Note that knowledge is lost in the logical schema representation. In particular, the inheritance associations have been obscured, thus requiring that a user impose an appropriate semantic interpretation. On the other hand, explicit associations in the semantic data model representation can be used to reduce logical level ambiguity.

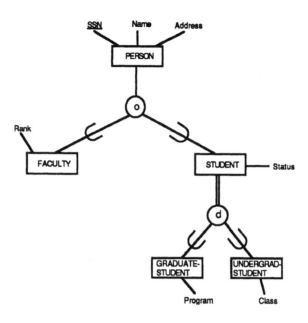

Fig. 2. Representing generalization.

3 Representing Context

While the rich representation constructs supported by a semantic data model provide a designer with the ability to represent complex domains, the mapping to the logical level results in the filtering of knowledge that may be useful for purposes other than design, such as automated query formulation over a universal relation interface and semantic query optimization. Even when a conceptual schema is available, additional constructs are required to realize desired information retrieval functionality.

To illustrate the need for higher level semantic constructs, consider a request to list the names of customers at the Columbia branch who have balances greater than $10,000:

```
Select   Customer-Name,
         Balance
Where    Balance > 10000   and
         Branch-Name = "Columbia"
```

The notation used in this request is referred to as USQL, as it is an SQL-like language for a universal relation interface. Specifically, a USQL request does not require (a) the qualification of attributes by relation names, (b) a FROM clause, or (c) the specification of natural join criteria.

Formulating a semantically valid query for the above request using only the logical schema requires some effort, even if a user is familiar with the schema. On the other hand, the ER diagram of Figure 1 explicitly delineates valid navigational paths that cover the requested attributes. For the example, it makes sense to use the path from CUSTOMER through ACCOUNT to BRANCH. Mapping this path to the logical level results in the following SQL query:

```
SELECT
        customer.customer-name,
        account.balance
FROM
        customer,
        customer-account,
        account,
        branch
WHERE
        account.balance >
          10000   AND
        branch.branch-name =
          "Columbia"   AND
        customer.ssn =
          customer-account.ssn   AND
        customer-account.account-id =
          account.account-id   AND
        account.branch-name =
          branch.branch-name
```

To generate the semantically valid query above, the formulator had to rule out the semantically unreasonable path through LOAN. Armed with appropriate domain and conceptual schema knowledge, this is a straightforward task. However, the task is not as straightforward if a user has less conceptual schema knowledge or less domain knowledge, or if there are many highly connected entity types for which multiple paths appear valid.

3.1   Inferring Likely Intent

When composing a request, a user employs mental models of both the domain represented by the database and the structure of the database itself. If the semantic gap between these two models is wide, query formulation is difficult. Unfortunately, the gap between a logical schema and a user's domain model typically is wide. On the other hand, the gap between a conceptual schema and a user's domain is narrower. However, even with this narrower gap, a user must map from his own domain model to the designer's conceptual model. As the views of a user and a designer may not coincide, simply providing a conceptual schema for navigation is not appropriate. Instead, an intelligent interface should shield the user from both the conceptual and logical schemas.

One approach for shielding users from the underlying database details is based on the universal relation interface [8, 18]. However, this approach requires the use of abstractions, such as hypergraphs and maximal objects, that typically are not used by designers, thus complicating design efforts. An alternative approach is to use the conceptual schema directly, segmenting the ER graph into overlapping subgraphs of strongly associated conceptual level objects. If the conceptual design is sufficiently rich, the subgraphs, which will be referred to as *contexts*, should correspond to user intent. A valid request, then, will map to one or more contexts, and an invalid request will not map to any context.

Consider again the banking example in Figure 1. In this example, it does not make sense to follow the apparent navigational paths that exist between ACCOUNT and LOAN, as these imply natural join queries exist that relate the two entities. On the other hand, there do appear to be valid natural join paths between CUSTOMER and BRANCH. Thus, as shown in Figure 3, at least two contexts exist.

3.2   Finding Contexts Automatically

While contexts can be identified manually, this is difficult to do when the ER model is large and complex. However, by using some basic heuristics, contexts can be identified automatically. As is discussed in the next section, the generated contexts can, in turn, be refined manually. The principal idea underlying ER object inclusion in a context is based on the notion of a lossless join. In particular, recall that a natural join between two relations R_1 and R_2 is lossless if the intersection of R_1 and R_2 functionally determines (or multidetermines) either R_1 or R_2 [9]. Abstracting this result to the conceptual level, two ER objects are strongly associated if their corresponding relations can be natural joined in a lossless way.

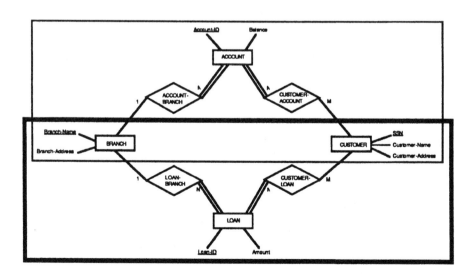

Fig. 3. Context diagram for banking example.

Considering the basic ER model and basing context inclusion on the lossless join property leads to the following inductive definition of a context:

Basis: A relationship type and its participating entity types is a context. This follows from the fact that a relationship set is conceptually a subset of the cartesian product of its participating entity sets. Therefore, a functional dependency must hold between the relationship set and its participating entity sets, as a relationship maps to one of each of its participating entities.

Induction: If C is a context and an N:1 or 1:1 relationship type R exists from an entity type in C to an entity type E not in C, then C $\cup$ {R} $\cup$ E is a context. This follows from the fact that N:1 and 1:1 relationship types imply that a localized functional dependency exists between two entity types. For example, the N:1 relationship type between ACCOUNT and BRANCH implies that ACCOUNT-ID functionally determines the attributes of BRANCH.

Note that the inductive step avoids cycles in contexts. Intuitively, this makes sense as the natural join of the relations corresponding to a cycle of ER objects results in an intersection relation. However, if such a relation were desired at the ER level, it would be represented by an n-ary relationship type. Further justification for including ER objects in contexts as well as other rules dealing with basic ER model constructs (e.g., recursive relationship types and acyclic ER graph extensions) are described by Semmel [14].

Constructing a set of conceptual schema contexts entails creating contexts via the inductive definition above, and then eliminating contexts that are subgraphs of other contexts. These subsumed contexts can be recreated by pruning the remaining contexts.

To demonstrate automatic context generation, consider the contexts produced for the banking example of Figure 1 by the basis of the context definition:

```
C1:  (ACCOUNT, ACCOUNT-BRANCH, BRANCH)
C2:  (LOAN, CUSTOMER-LOAN, CUSTOMER)
C3:  (CUSTOMER, CUSTOMER-ACCOUNT, ACCOUNT)
C4:  (BRANCH, LOAN-BRANCH, LOAN)
```

By the inductive step, contexts C1 and C2 cannot be extended, as doing so would require pushing through either M:N or 1:N relationship types. However, contexts C3 and C4 can be extended resulting in the following set of contexts:

```
C1:   (ACCOUNT, ACCOUNT-BRANCH, BRANCH)
C2:   (LOAN, CUSTOMER-LOAN, CUSTOMER)
C3':  (CUSTOMER, CUSTOMER-ACCOUNT, ACCOUNT, ACCOUNT-BRANCH,
       BRANCH)
C4':  (BRANCH, LOAN-BRANCH, LOAN, CUSTOMER-LOAN, CUSTOMER)
```

At this point, no context can be extended. Moreover, as context c_3' subsumes context c_1, c_1 can be eliminated. Similarly, c_2 can be eliminated. Thus, the two contexts that were shown in Figure 3 remain.

To deal with inheritance hierarchies, the notion of lossless join must be generalized. In particular, a natural join among members in an inheritance hierarchy makes sense only if a null relation cannot be guaranteed. For example, it makes sense to allow joins between relations corresponding to a subclass and a superclass as all subclass entities are associated with a superclass entity. Similarly, relations corresponding to overlapping subclasses can be natural joined as there may be common entities. However, it does not make sense to join subclasses under a disjoint generalization type.

To illustrate how contexts are created with simple inheritance hierarchies, consider again the university hierarchy shown in Figure 2. In this case, three initial contexts can be formulated:

```
C1:    (FACULTY, STUDENT, PERSON)
C2:    (GRADUATE-STUDENT, STUDENT)
C3:    (UNDERGRAD-STUDENT, STUDENT)
```

Context c_1 is justified by the overlapping generalization type from PERSON to both FACULTY and STUDENT. On the other hand, contexts c_2 and c_3 must be distinct because of the disjoint generalization type. At this point, contexts can be extended. Analyzing the structure of the conceptual schema, it is not possible to rule out the possibility that both graduate and undergraduate students can be faculty members. Consequently, context c_1 can be merged with contexts c_2 and c_3 resulting in the final set of contexts:

```
C2':    (GRADUATE-STUDENT, STUDENT, FACULTY, PERSON)
C3':    (UNDERGRAD-STUDENT, STUDENT, FACULTY, PERSON)
```

4 Using Design Knowledge for Retrieval

Contexts extend the ER model, and can be used to automate query formulation. The basic approach is to find contexts that cover the requested attributes, prune the found contexts to eliminate extraneous ER objects, map the pruned contexts to relations, and generate the final query. It also is possible to semantically optimize the resultant query by minimizing the number of joins that will be required. Such optimization exploits the structural characteristics of the underlying ER conceptual schema as well as the mapping from the conceptual schema to the logical schema.

4.1 Query Formulation with Contexts

To demonstrate context-based query formulation, consider a USQL request to list the balances of accounts managed by the Columbia branch:

```
Select   Account-ID,
         Balance
Where    Branch-Name = "Columbia"
```

First all contexts that cover the requested attributes are found. For the example, only the top context applies (in general, multiple contexts may apply):

```
(CUSTOMER, CUSTOMER-ACCOUNT, ACCOUNT, ACCOUNT-BRANCH, BRANCH)
```

The found context then is pruned by continually eliminating leaves until every leaf covers requested attributes. In the example, the ER objects CUSTOMER and CUSTOMER-ACCOUNT are pruned resulting in the following context:

```
(ACCOUNT, ACCOUNT-BRANCH, BRANCH)
```

Next, the remaining context ER objects are placed in a natural join order, as indicated by explicit conceptual schema edges, and mapped to relation schemas. In the example, the ER objects already are in natural join order. However, ACCOUNT-BRANCH is represented by a foreign key in the relation schema ACCOUNT, thus resulting in duplicate relations after the conceptual level ER objects are mapped to logical level relation objects:

```
(ACCOUNT, ACCOUNT, BRANCH)
```

As natural joining a relation with itself produces the original relation, duplicate relation schemas are eliminated:

```
(ACCOUNT, BRANCH)
```

The last step is to generate the final query. This requires knowledge of the mapping from the conceptual schema to the logical schema so that appropriate natural join criteria will be used. The final query is as follows:

```
SELECT
        account.account-id
        account.balance
FROM
        account,
        branch
WHERE
        branch.branch-name =
          "Columbia"  AND
        account.branch-name =
          branch.branch-name
```

4.2   Semantic Query Optimization

While the above query will produce the correct result, it is not the query that a database expert would formulate. Rather, the expert would recognize that the attribute BRANCH-NAME exists in the relation ACCOUNT as a foreign key and could be qualified directly, thus avoiding the natural join. To achieve this result automatically requires more intelligent processing of the pruned contexts. Specifically, semantic query optimization is required.

Recall that a query optimizer attempts to transform a query so that it will execute more efficiently. Conventional query optimizers focus on algebraic manipulation of a query tree corresponding to a query [6]. Thus, the optimizations tend to be syntactic in nature, as they are independent of the semantics of the database over which they are applied. Less common is the transformation of a query into a form in which a different set of relations is used. This requires semantic query optimization that focuses on semantic constraints (e.g., referential integrity constraints) that hold over the database [7, 15].

Using only conceptual schema knowledge, it is impossible to determine that the natural join in the example above is superfluous, as attributes are not duplicated at the conceptual level. However, by using knowledge of the mapping from the conceptual schema to the logical schema, it is possible to semantically optimize the query so that the natural join is avoided. In particular, the mapping supports referential integrity among the relations corresponding to a relationship set and its participating entity sets. As a result, if all of the request attributes covered by an entity type are key, that entity type can be eliminated and the relation corresponding to the relationship type can be used in its place; this is called the *unnecessary entity type deletion rule* [13].

In the example, all requested attributes are key. Thus, the pruned context can be further pruned via the unnecessary entity type deletion rule. However, to identify from which relations the requested attributes will be drawn, the optimized context must be annotated. One way to annotate a context is to introduce virtual entity types that (a) indicate which underlying relation to use for entity key attributes, and (b) maintain ER representation consistency so that further optimization can occur. For the example, the following optimized context is produced:

```
(VIRTUAL-ACCOUNT, ACCOUNT-BRANCH, VIRTUAL-BRANCH)
```

Upon mapping to relation schemas, the virtual entity types are eliminated (after informing the query formulator where key attributes will be found) and the relationship type ACCOUNT-BRANCH is mapped to the relation schema ACCOUNT:

```
(ACCOUNT)
```

At this point, the final query can be generated:

```
SELECT
        account.account-id
```

```
        account.balance
FROM
        account
WHERE
        account.branch-name =
          "Columbia"
```

The unnecessary entity type deletion rule can have dramatic effects if only key attributes are being requested. In addition, similar rules exist that can be applied to weak entity types. These rules can be generalized to work with inheritance hierarchies. In fact, the exhaustive application of these rules guarantees that a query will use the fewest relations, thereby minimizing the number of joins required [13]. For real-world databases, such minimization usually results in an efficient execution strategy.

To illustrate how semantic query optimization works with hierarchies, consider a request over the university example of Figure 2 to list the names of all students who are seniors:

```
Select  Name
Where   Class = "Senior"
```

The context applying to this query is as follows:

```
(UNDERGRAD-STUDENT, STUDENT, FACULTY, PERSON)
```

After initial pruning, the following context is produced:

```
(UNDERGRAD-STUDENT, STUDENT, PERSON)
```

While a query now could be formulated, the semantic query optimizer can exploit the fact that all undergraduate students are persons. This enables the optimizer to eliminate the join through STUDENT, which results in the following optimized context:

```
(UNDERGRAD-STUDENT, PERSON)
```

At this point, the final query can be generated:

```
SELECT
        person.name
FROM
        person,
        undergrad-student
WHERE   undergrad-student.class =
          "Senior"  AND
        person.ssn =
          undergrad-student.ssn
```

5 The QUICK System and Design Feedback

A prototype system has been constructed that implements the ideas presented above. QUICK (which stands for "QUICK is a Universal Interface with Conceptual Knowledge") processes the textual description of an ER conceptual schema to produce a logical schema. Details, such as attribute renaming for recursive relationship types or multiple N:1 relationship types between two entity types, are handled via directed interaction with the designer. Once the ER model has been processed, QUICK automatically generates contexts. While the worst case running time of context generation is an exponential function of the number of entity types, QUICK exploits real-world design constraints to keep the running time manageable [13]. Finally, QUICK accepts high-level requests and generates SQL.

To demonstrate the validity of QUICK, a large ER conceptual schema for the catalog section of the Data Archive and Distribution System (DADS) of the Space Telescope Science Institute was used. DADS has been designed to store astronomical data returned by the Hubble Space Telescope. When initially input to QUICK, the DADS catalog design consisted of 27 entity types and 31 relationship types [4]. Using a Macintosh IIfx, processing of the DADS ER design took less than five seconds. Creation of contexts took approximately five minutes; as context creation need be done only when the conceptual design is created or modified, this running time is acceptable. Queries for all requests were generated in approximately one second. High-level requests ranged in length from one to seven lines, while generated SQL queries ranged in length from 10 to more than 200 lines. Examples are shown in [13] and [14].

While the generated queries were deemed semantically valid by a designer, one query initially caused concerns. In particular, the query consisted of the union of five subqueries. Each subquery corresponded to a different context, and QUICK determined that the likely intent was represented by a union. Upon inspection, each subquery made sense. This led to an evaluation of the conceptual schema, and a flaw in the design was discovered. Specifically, extraneous relationship types had been established among various entity types. Eliminating these relationship types resulted in a valid query that consisted of two subqueries.

Upon discovering the problematic query, but before searching for design flaws, the initial reaction was that the context generation algorithm was not appropriate for the DADS database, and, therefore, contexts had to be created manually. However, upon discovering the design flaw, it became apparent that QUICK could serve as a design tool as well as an information retrieval tool. In particular, QUICK supports two methods for identifying potential anomalies in a conceptual schema:

1. Contexts can be evaluated manually. As a context is a high-level semantic construct that groups strongly associated ER objects, a knowledgeable designer can determine if a context corresponds to a reasonable conceptual schema subgraph. A shortcoming of this approach is that a large and complex ER graph may have large contexts, and it could be difficult to evaluate all

contexts. In DADS, for example, there were 11 contexts, and each context contained on the order of 50 ER objects.

2. High-level requests can be posed, and resultant queries can be evaluated. When a problem is discovered, the design can be evaluated and modified appropriately. The advantage of this approach is that the search for problems can be driven by typical requests, and problems can be resolved in a directed manner by analyzing the specific contexts that were used to formulate the problematic query.

Contexts thus provide a mechanism for testing the soundness of a conceptual design. Limited real-world experience with QUICK indicates that problems most likely will be discovered when invalid queries are formulated. These queries should lead to an evaluation of the conceptual schema. If design flaws are discovered, the conceptual schema can be modified, contexts can be regenerated, and the query corresponding to the problematic request can be reformulated. This process can iterate until the queries generated are valid, or until the designer feels that no more changes to the conceptual schema are justified. In the latter case, if invalid queries continue to be generated, contexts can be handcrafted, with the generated contexts serving as a useful starting point.

6 Summary and Conclusions

The conceptual schema is a valuable knowledge resource that can be used throughout an information system's life cycle. Serving initially in a design role, the conceptual schema also can be used to support query formulation, semantic query optimization, and design feedback. To realize these capabilities, contexts have been introduced as a means for segmenting ER graphs into overlapping subgraphs of strongly associated conceptual objects. Although contexts may be viewed as an extension of the ER model, in most cases they can be inferred from ER structural characteristics. When necessary, contexts can be handcrafted to correspond to the semantics of the domain modeled by the information system.

Current research is focused on the use of richer conceptual schema constructs (e.g., inheritance constructs that allow intermingling of overlapping and disjoint subclasses). In addition to facilitating the representation of complex domains, the richer constructs enhance the ability of the context generator to determine when a conceptual level object should be included in a context. The constructs also can be used effectively for semantic query optimization.

Finally, research is being conducted on how to use contexts as knowledge constructs that can be augmented. For example, it is possible to associate arbitrary predicates with a context to determine if it should be used in the formulation of a query corresponding to a request. Such predicates can incorporate significant knowledge, including user model knowledge and intercontext constraints. Combined with richer conceptual schema constructs, context augmentation will facilitate the creation of high-level and intelligent interfaces.

7 References

1. C. Batini, B. Ceri, S. B. Navathe: Conceptual Database Design: An Entity-Relationship Approach. Redwood City, CA: Benjamin/Cummings 1992

2. P. P. Chen: The Entity-Relationship Model - Toward a Unified View of Data. ACM Transactions on Database Systems 1:1, 9-36 (1976)

3. R. Elmasri, S. B. Navathe: Fundamentals of Database Systems. Reading, MA: Addison-Wesley 1989

4. Ford Aerospace Corporation: Appendix B to User's Guide for the Space Telescope Data Archive and Distribution Service (ST DADS) CDR Version. Ford Aerospace Corporation Space Programs Operation, October 1990

5. R. Hull, R. King: Semantic Database Modeling: Survey, Applications, and Research Issues. ACM Computing Surveys 19:3, 201-260 (1987)

6. M. Jarke, J. Koch: Query Optimization in Database Systems. ACM Computing Surveys 16:2, 111-152 (1984)

7. J. J. King: QUIST: A System for Semantic Query Optimization in Relational Databases. In: Proceedings of the 7th International Conference on Very Large Data Bases, 1981, pp. 510-517

8. H. F. Korth, G. M. Kuper, J. Feigenbaum, A. Van Gelder, J. D. Ullman: System/U: A Database System Based on the Universal Relation Assumption. ACM Transactions on Database Systems 9:3, 331-347 (1984)

9. H. F. Korth, A. Silberschatz: Database System Concepts, 2nd ed. New York: McGraw-Hill 1991

10. D. Maier, J. D. Ullman: Maximal Objects and the Semantics of Universal Relation Databases. ACM Transactions on Database Systems 8:1, 1-14 (1983)

11. D. Maier, J. D. Ullman, M. Y. Vardi: On the Foundations of the Universal Relation Model. ACM Transactions on Database Systems 9:2, 283-308 (1984)

12. J. Mylopoulos, H. J. Levesque: An Overview of Knowledge Representation. In: M. L. Brodie, J. Mylopoulos, J. W. Schmidt (eds.): On Conceptual Modelling: Perspectives from Artificial Intelligence, Databases, and Programming Languages. New York: Springer-Verlag 1984, pp. 3-17

13. R. D. Semmel: A Knowledge-Based Approach to Automated Query Formulation. Ph.D. Dissertation. Baltimore: University of Maryland 1991

14. R. D. Semmel: A Knowledge-Based System for Automated Query Formulation. In: Proceedings of the Fifth Florida Artificial Intelligence Research Symposium, 1992, pp. 80-84

15. S. T. Shenoy, Z. M. Ozsoyoglu: A System for Semantic Query Optimization. In: Proceedings 1987 ACM SIGMOD International Conference on Management of Data, 1987, pp. 181-195

16. J. M. Smith, D. C. P. Smith: Database Abstractions: Aggregation and Generalization. ACM Transactions on Database Systems 2:2, 105-133 (1977)

17. T. J. Teory, D. Yang, J. P. Fry: A Logical Design Methodology for Relational Databases Using the Extended Entity-Relationship Model. ACM Computing Surveys 18:2, 197-222 (1986)

18. J. D. Ullman: Universal Relation Interfaces for Database Systems. In: Proceedings of the IFIP 9th World Computer Congress, 1983, pp. 243-252

19. J. D. Ullman: Principles of Database and Knowledge-Base Systems, Vol. 2. Rockville, MD: Computer Science Press 1989

An Interactive Image Management System for Face Information Retrieval

Jeffrey R. Bach, Santanu Paul, and Ramesh Jain*

Artificial Intelligence Laboratory, Computer Science and Engineering, University of Michigan, Ann Arbor, MI 48109

Abstract. The complex nature of two-dimensional image data has presented problems for traditional information systems designed strictly for alpha-numeric data. In many systems, images are simply treated as an additional data type, making no use of the actual image data. However, this image data provides an enormous amount of information and should be utilized for more powerful retrieval capabilities. In this paper we present a general system architecture for image management systems which combines the strengths of computer vision systems with traditional information management techniques. This system will provide a general framework for the development of any domain-specific application. Our approach utilizes computer vision routines for both insertion and retrieval, and allows easy query-by-example specifications. The vision routines are used to segment and evaluate images based on descriptions of the domain objects and their attributes. The vision system can then assign feature values to be used for similarity-measures and image retrieval. An image management system developed for face-image retrieval is presented to demonstrate these ideas.

1 Introduction

In recent years much emphasis has been placed on developing systems which make effective use of multi-dimensional data. This data may take the form of images, graphics, video sequences, satellite images, and other scientific data. Many fields are dependent upon this type of data, but few systems have made effective use of the actual contents of the data. This data has presented problems for traditional information systems which are not prepared to handle anything beyond standard alpha-numeric data. The new multi-media and image-management systems must provide the ability to handle this data with the effectiveness with which traditional information systems manage their data. Processes for interpretation, maintenance, and retrieval must be developed to allow effective management of this complex data.

Current image management systems have yet to take advantage of the descriptive power of the actual image data. These systems lack the most important

---

* Supported by NSF grant NSF-IRI-9110683.

feature of visual information systems: the ability to analyze and retrieve images based on actual image contents. The system must allow a user to specify queries using actual image-data and image interpretations in addition to the standard textual descriptions. This process is typically called Query-By-Example (QBE). By allowing queries to be specified with actual image data, more complex queries can be generated with greater ease. A user will not have to rely on his interpretation of complex data in order to retrieve the intended data. However, this is not a process of simply matching a query image with a stored image. The user should be given this QBE ability as a tool to generate queries using portions of actual images, multiple images, varying-degrees of image-similarity, and standard alpha-numeric descriptions. Our QBE retrieval process makes use of the same vision processes that are used at the time of image-insertion, to provide consistent image interpretation. Our iterative query process also allows easy interactive QBE specifications. These ideas are first discussed in general terms, then implemented in a system for face-image retrieval.

The architecture we are discussing here emphasizes the notion of QBE to allow maximum flexibility in retrieving the desired images. We combine the strengths of computer vision systems and standard database systems as shown in figure 1, to take advantage of the benefits of each.

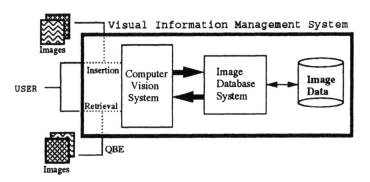

Fig. 1. Combining image databases and computer vision systems.

2 The VIMSYS Data Model

The VIMSYS data model [4] has provided the basis for the representation and storage of image data in our system. The data model provides a hierarchy of image representations based on the degree of semantic information associated with each representation. Following is a brief description of the four layers used in the data model.

– The **Domain event** layer defines relationships between specific domain object instances. These events can represent any relationship (for example, temporal or spatial) between any domain object instances. A typical domain event is the motion of a specific object.

– The **Domain object** layer maintains the real-world objects that exist in the specified domain. These represent the *important* objects that are managed by the application. Typical domain objects for a face-image application would be the face, the mouth, and so on.

– The **Image object** layer maintains the objects extracted from the images. These objects actually exist in the image, and are extracted through various segmentation processes. Image objects may correspond to occurrences of domain objects in an image. Typical image objects are regions and curves.

– The **Image representation** level is the "lowest" level of the hierarchy. This level maintains the actual image data, such as pixel coordinates, that comprises the image objects.

Each instance at a given layer can access the instances associated with it at the layers immediately above and below its layer. Thus, given a specific image object, it is easy to access the domain object to which it corresponds, as well as the actual image data which comprises it. This provides an effective means for locating specific instances of any data type, given a description of an instance at a specific layer. The importance of this hierarchy will become more apparent as various aspects of our system are presented.

3 System Architecture

The architecture discussed here has been designed to allow different applications to be developed and implemented in a consistent way. The system itself is comprised of four main components, as shown in figure 2. Each component is briefly described here. Subsequent sections will describe their structure and function in more detail.

– **Image database.** This component provides the storage mechanism for the actual image data as well as the features which the images contain. Each feature that is evaluated at the time of insertion is stored in the database with its computed value and a reference to the image containing it. Similarly, every image in the database references the features which it contains. This corresponds to the VIMSYS data model discussed above, which allows well-defined relationships between the actual images, image features, and the real-world domain objects which they represent.

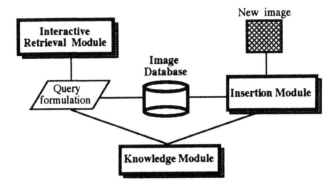

Fig. 2. Relationship of system components

- **Insertion module.** This component allows the insertion and evaluation of images into the database. It is during these processes that values will be computed for all the important features in the image. Although it is desirable for this insertion process to be entirely automatic, there are several limitations to this type of approach. Many domains consist of poorly defined objects and features which are difficult to accurately evaluate in many cases. Allowing the user to alter or override the results when necessary will provide much more accurate data than an automatic system, and much more convenience than a totally manual approach.

- **Retrieval module.** This module is used interactively by the user to retrieve information from the database. Queries may be either completely user-specified, or generated based on the results of previous queries. The latter type is constructed from characteristics of actual images retrieved for the user. The system then translates these characteristics into specific feature values. This allows the user to query based on the contents of other images, without forcing him to know the actual values of the features. This is very important since most feature values will be in terms of low-level image attributes such as pixel intensity values. After the results of the query are displayed, the user can generate a new query either by using the contents of these new images, specifying new feature values, or both.

- **Domain Knowledge module.** This component maintains all the domain-specific information that must be maintained for each specific application. This information is utilized by every process in the system. Domain object descriptions are used to segment the necessary features in new images. These features are then stored in the database, using the specified representational scheme. During the retrieval process, user-specified descriptions must be mapped into relevant feature values. Information about altering feature values, and evaluating the *similarity* of features and images is also maintained. The aspects of this system that pertain specifically to the chosen domain are represented by this knowledge, which insures a separation of the general architecture from the specific domain. This allows the architecture to serve as a general platform for development of other applications.

These ideas are being used to develop an interactive system for the retrieval of face images and information. The system will allow users to retrieve the identity and any additional information about a person they describe. The user will create and alter the description by actually describing individual facial features, or by describing the features in terms of actual image data from other face images. Faces satisfying the given description will then be retrieved. The description can be iteratively modified until the desired face has been located. This process allows images to be retrieved based on feature-similarity values of actual image data.

4 Image Database

In order to store an image in the system, all the information associated with the image must be stored in the database. Actual objects in the image and image regions cannot simply be stored the way standard information is stored. For example, a group of pixels forming an object in an image must be stored in the database, but it would be very impractical to store each of the individual pixel coordinates. The data must be put into a form which is easy to manage, yet still represents the object in the image.

4.1 Feature representation

When an object is identified in an image, it must be translated into a more efficient representation to be stored in the database. This internal representation is used to maintain the necessary information about each domain object in the database. It reduces storage costs and makes the important information much more accessible. The available representation schemes will be maintained by the system in the *Representation Scheme Library*, along with the procedures to translate an object in an image to its corresponding representation. In the following section we will discuss the mechanism for selecting which attributes the corresponding representation scheme must represent. This representation will actually provide the mapping between the three levels of the VIMSYS model [4]. Each domain object D that is located in an image I will be associated with an image object O, which provides the necessary representation of D. These mappings provide a convenient mechanism for content-based queries and image-based queries, as will be seen in section 6.

As domain objects become more complex, comparing their actual image data will become more difficult. Thus, the stored image representations of the objects must be used to compare the similarity of different objects. This means that all the characteristics which help differentiate object instances must be incorporated into the representation scheme.

By maintaining a library of representation transformations at the system level, instead of with each individual domain object, several objects can make use of general representation schemes. This allows different applications built on the same framework of this project to utilize predefined image objects and transformations whenever convenient. This mechanism also provides the ability to easily change which characteristics of an object are important by altering the internal representation scheme which it uses. Thus, the domain objects and features can be easily refined without any other alterations to the system.

5   Image Insertion

This component is responsible for determining values for all information that is to be stored in the database. When new images are inserted into the system, the necessary objects and attributes must be evaluated and stored. This process must make use of the domain object descriptions, which will provide the information necessary to locate and segment the objects that exist in the image.

5.1   Domain object descriptions

When an image management system is developed for a specific application, the objects and features that are important in that application can be specified *a priori*. Vision routines can then be designed which work very effectively on these specific features. However, it is also beneficial to allow the user to define objects and attributes without requiring complex vision routines to be designed. This requires a mechanism for defining the objects and their attributes that are necessary for a chosen application. These domain object descriptions must provide enough information to locate the object in an image and evaluate the necessary attributes. These attributes will be used to represent the object in the database, and compute the similarity between object instances during the retrieval process. To create these descriptions, the user is given the the the following options:

- **Attribute specifications** are used to indicate values and constraints for attributes which are easily described with a number or range of numbers. This will provide the basic information that is required of all domain object descriptions.

- **Graphical tools** are used to provide more complex shape information about a specific domain object. This option allows the user to provide more detailed shape information than can be provided with the previous option. These tools allow the user to sketch particular shapes, indicate unusual attributes (such as a specific distance or angle), or graphically assign values and ranges to the standard attributes. It should be noted that the actual sketch will *not* be used as a template for the object. Instead, the sketch is combined with the other specified attribute values to create the object description that will be used during the segmentation process.

- **Object relationships** give the user the ability to define relationships between individual components of an object, or between different object types. These relationships also allow a user to create *composite objects* comprised of previously defined domain objects. A simple example utilizing these relationships will be discussed in the context of the face image application.

For simple, poorly-defined objects, only the global attributes are necessary to represent the object. As objects become more complex and consistent (i.e. little variance between instances), more local features will be required to accurately represent this object. The two types of features (global vs. local) will tend to be used in different tasks. The global features will be more useful in distinguishing between different domain object classes, while the local features will be more useful when comparing instances of the same class. The amount of global and local information that must be captured for a specific domain object will dictate how instances of the object must be represented in the database. For example, a domain object class which does not possess a consistent shape requirement may be identified using only the area and intensity of the region. In this case, only the location, area, and intensity need to be stored to accurately represent instances of this object type. On the other hand, objects with a very intricate shape requirement must be represented in a way which is much more sensitive to local features, such as a *B-spline* representation.

5.2 Domain feature types

For every domain object type D_k that is defined in an application, there is a corresponding set of attributes $A_k = \{a_{k,1}, a_{k,2}, ...a_{k,l}\}$ which define this object. For each application, the set of *features* that are necessary, is the collection of these individual attributes for each domain object D_k. Each individual feature, f_i, can be classified into one of the following classes, depending on how its value is determined.

1. F_u. This set contains the features which are *user-specified*. Values are assigned by the user at the time of insertion.
2. F_d. This set contains the features which are *derived* directly from the image data, and calculated at the time of insertion.
3. F_c. This set contains the features whose values are not computed until they are needed. Routines must be provided to compute these values when they become necessary.

User-specified feature values. Automatic image segmentation is a very desirable feature in an image management system, because of the great convenience it provides. However, it is also necessary to attach other semantic, non-derivable data to the images. This set of *user-specified* features, labelled $\mathbf{F_u}$, is used to provide additional information about the image. For example, in a face image application, the user must supply personnel information, such as **name** and **id number**, which cannot be automatically extracted from the image.

Derived-feature values. This section will discuss the processes of evaluating and storing features of type f_d. Each of these features will be located and evaluated during the segmentation process when the image is inserted. This segmentation will occur in two phases: the *general* segmentation and the *domain* segmentation.

The purpose of the general segmentation phase is to segment the image into general image objects. This is done without utilizing the domain object descriptions supplied by the user. The importance of this segmentation process is that image objects (such as *regions* and *curves*) will be available later on, without re-segmenting the image. This will eliminate much of the computation that is required when a new object or feature is used in a query. The images will not have to be re-segmented in order to locate the necessary objects. The objects resulting from this process correspond to the *image object* layer of the VIMSYS model. The next step of segmentation will determine which *domain objects* exist in the image, and will associate each with its corresponding image object.

The domain segmentation process will use the segmented image to locate and evaluate the domain objects in the image. This is based on the domain object descriptions supplied by the user. The specified attribute values of each domain object type will be used to determine to which image objects (if any) they correspond. The initial information required for the domain segmentation will be supplied by the *occurrence* attributes such as absolute location, relative location, and required number of occurrences. This information, along with global shape information, such as gross shape and area, can provide enough information to determine the existence of a particular object type, as long as the domain object types are not too similar. As domain object classes become more similar, more local shape information must be used to determine the correct object type.

When a specific image object is associated with a domain object, a segmentation certainty value, Seg_i, will be computed to represent how well the image object satisfies the feature f_i of the domain object description. Each feature f_i of type $\mathbf{F_d}$ also has a value Seg_i^{min} associated with it to indicate the threshold value for accepting this evaluation of f_i. If the given segmentation does not satisfy the requirements of a domain object description with an acceptable degree of certainty, $Seg_i \leq Seg_i^{min}$, the image object is not considered an instance of this domain object. All features, including absolute location, relative location, and number of occurrences, will be evaluated this way. If an acceptable domain segmentation is not achieved, the total segmentation is re-computed, starting with the general segmentation. However, the parameters used in the general segmentation will be altered to provide a different set of image objects than the previous attempt. For example, the subsequent general segmentation may result in a larger number of image objects, to account for domain objects which could not be located. So in effect, the general segmentation can be directly affected by the domain object descriptions. Once the segmentation satisfies the constraints of the domain object descriptions, the segmentation is complete, and the object instances are stored in the database using their corresponding representation schemes.

Computable features. Features of the type $\mathbf{F}_c$ are those which are rarely used during query processing, or which are very costly to compute. The first time a feature $f_i \in \mathbf{F}_c$ is required, the appropriate processes will calculate this value and store it for future use. In order to make this process as efficient as possible, image objects resulting from the general segmentation are used when new features are encountered. That is, for each image object $\mathbf{IO}_j$ representing domain object $\mathbf{D}_j$, a region $\mathbf{R}_j$ of the original image will be stored which provides access to the actual image data of $\mathbf{IO}_j$. This corresponds to the *image representation* layer of the VIMSYS model. With easy access to $\mathbf{IO}_j$ and $\mathbf{R}_j$, the problem of computing the features $\mathbf{F}_c$ becomes somewhat simpler. It is not necessary to relocate and evaluate the desired object in the image. Consider $f_i \in \mathbf{F}_c$, which is a new attribute of $\mathbf{D}_j$. If the new feature can be computed using only the stored attributes of $\mathbf{IO}_j$, the actual image data will not be necessary. If the stored representation does not provide enough information, the region $\mathbf{R}_j$ in the image can be examined to compute the value of f_i. Thus, the cost of re-segmenting the image is still avoided.

6 Image Retrieval

This mechanism involves several processes, each of which is described in more detail below. Object-specific knowledge, as well as knowledge in the form of user-intervention, is incorporated in each step of the process. When a query session is begun, initial values must be assigned to those features which the user has described. Whenever a user specifies a certain feature value to be altered, the system must modify this value based on the global statistics of that feature, and on the relative magnitude of change specified by the user. The calculated feature values for an image are then submitted as a query to retrieve those images which satisfy the feature-value specifications. The images which are then determined to be *most similar* are presented to the user.

6.1 Initial feature specification

When a user initiates a search for an image, all features specified by the user will be given an initial feature value based on the statistics for that feature. The feature is initially described in terms which are meaningful to the user. The corresponding domain knowledge will then provide a mapping from the user specified term, to an actual value for that feature. Thus, when terms such as *wide* or *dark* are chosen to describe a feature, a value will be calculated for that feature based on the magnitude specified by the user, and the amount of variance for that feature in the system. Since actual feature values are often meaningless to the user or cumbersome to work with, it is important to provide this type of mechanism to allow the user to accurately describe the desired data. This initial assignment is shown in figure 3.

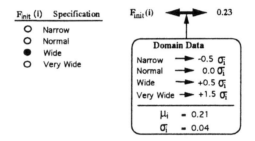

Fig. 3. Example mapping of initial user-specification to actual feature value.

6.2 Feature-value alteration

After this initial query is executed and the most similar images are returned, the user may generate subsequent queries with attribute values based on these results. This allows the user to specify relative values such as *narrower*, *wider*, and *much wider* which provides an effective mechanism for specifying feature values based on actual image contents. This also allows the user to systematically refine feature descriptions until satisfactory results are obtained. The amount that feature values are changed in response to an alteration is similar to the calculation for the initial values described above.

$$f'(i) = f(i) + \Delta_u(i) * \sigma_i \quad \text{where}$$

$f(i)$ is the current value of feature i
$f'(i)$ is the resulting value of feature i
$\Delta_u(i)$ is the *relative feature-value* change, as described below
σ_i is the standard deviation for feature i

The value $\Delta_u(i)$ is defined as:

$$\Delta_u(i) = \frac{\sigma_i \cdot K \cdot \delta_u}{N} C_i \quad \text{where}$$

σ_i is the standard deviation for feature i

K is the number of images to be returned to the user

δ_u is the magnitude of the change specified by the user for feature i (e.g. **much wider**)

N is the number of occurrences of feature f_i in the database

C_i is a constant used to scale the amount of change to the feature

The δ_u values will provide the ability to specify both drastic feature changes, as well as minimal changes. This is necessary in order to retrieve subsequent data with very little variation in a specific feature, from the displayed data to the desired data. The formula above shows that as the number of occurrences N of f_i increases, the amount of change $\Delta_u(i)$ will decrease. This is to avoid large changes in f_i that may step over the target values. However, a larger standard deviation σ_i will allow a larger change value in the feature f_i.

6.3 Image similarity

Once the individual feature values are specified, the system will retrieve the images *most similar* to this description. The similarity calculation is based on the individual feature values contained in the images. This is shown in more detail for face images in section 8.3.

6.4 Image-based queries

An important feature in image-based systems is the ability to query using actual image contents. This allows complex queries to be specified without requiring the user to specify values for each of the attributes involved. By utilizing the relationship between each domain object $\mathbf{D}_j$ and image object $\mathbf{IO}_j$, queries of this type become much easier to process. These relationships are important in queries of the following types:

Find all I which contain D_i

Find all D which are contained in I_j

These relationships also allow an effective mechanism for handling queries based on other images. For example, the query:

Find all I which contain a domain object *similar* to D_k of I_l

is processed by using the corresponding image object IO_k of D_k. It is this representation that maintains all the necessary information about D_k that is required for determining similarity values. Image objects which are similar to IO_k are then used to determine which domain objects must be retrieved.

7 Domain Knowledge Organization

Although specific processes and information will differ greatly between different domains, the *types* of information and the tasks required will be common to any application. The implementation of the knowledge module provides a consistent method for incorporating the domain-specific information into the system, while allowing a more general architecture to be developed. By recognizing this separation of knowledge, we will develop a system architecture which will not be limited to a specific domain.

Regardless of the domain or the objects chosen to represent the domain, certain aspects of how to process these objects must be maintained. Because of the consistent nature of the information that must be used for each object, development has been approached from basically an object-oriented point of view. The functions that make use of this knowledge can be divided into the three categories listed below:

- **Segmentation and Insertion Knowledge.** This involves the type of processing that is required to locate each object in an image. For each domain object, the necessary description will be maintained to allow this object to be identified and segmented in an image.

- **Representation Knowledge.** This determines how each domain object is to be represented in the database. The chosen representation of the domain object must be one that incorporates all the necessary information to distinguish this object from others of its type. The representation scheme for each object will actually provide a mapping between the different layers of the VIMSYS data model. The representation will determine which types of image objects each domain object may be associated with. The chosen representation will also be used for determining the similarity of objects, during the object retrieval process. This calculation would be difficult if only actual image data were available to represent the objects.

- **Query Knowledge.** This information is used during the processes of formulating and submitting queries, and evaluating the results. For each feature, initial descriptions must be specified which will then be translated into actual feature values. Information must also be provided to determine how these feature values are affected by factors such as the user's confidence in assigning a value to this feature. Once images are retrieved, additional knowledge must be used to rank the images by order of similarity. This makes use of information about the importance of each individual feature in differentiating between objects and images.

8   Face Information Retrieval

The application we have implemented to demonstrate these ideas is an interactive system for the retrieval of face images and information. The project allows a user to locate a specific person in the database, and retrieve the person's image and other relevant information. All the concepts of the previous sections have been incorporated into this project.

For any application, an understanding of the necessary objects and attributes is very important to the success of the system. In developing this project, we have relied very heavily on previous research in the field of face recognition. Much work has been done in the psychological aspects [1, 5, 6, 8, 14] which have provided a basis for our initial implementation. Many automatic face recognition systems have also been developed. Our project is not a face recognition system, but rather a visual information system used for interactive face retrieval. Some face-recognition systems have approached the problem from strictly an image processing point of view, with little or no emphasis on user interaction. The system described in [3] is used for automatically locating faces in images, while [2, 7, 12, 13] describe methods for recognizing a person stored in the database. Connectionist networks have also been implemented for recognizing faces [9, 11] and evaluating facial expressions. The FRAME system [10] actually incorporates database methods for indexing and similarity.

As in any image management application, we are faced with the difficulty of determining which attributes are important for each domain object, and how to accurately represent these features in the system. For instance, there are several attributes about an eye that may be important. Individual eye attributes such as area and width will be necessary, as will relative attributes such as the width of the eye compared to the height of the eye. Spatial attributes such as distance between the left eye and the right eye are also important and must be incorporated into the system. Other objects, such as eyebrows, may require entirely different attributes than those for eyes to be maintained in the system. We have based much of our initial implementation on research that has been done to evaluate which facial features and attributes are best suited for face identification and differentiation [1, 6]. The two main user processes of image *insertion* and image *retrieval* are described in the following sections.

8.1   Image Insertion

Before any images can be inserted into the database, domain object descriptions must be generated for the objects and attributes that are to be used. A simple example will be given to demonstrate the process. However, the representation and segmentation details will not be covered in this paper. Instead, we will emphasize the general processes involved for inserting images and interactively retrieving a specific image.

When a new face is entered into the database, all the necessary features must be located and evaluated. Although this process should be as automated as possible, facial objects cannot always be accurately computed. After the automatic processing is complete, the user is given the ability to alter the given results. Once satisfactory results are obtained, the image data and corresponding feature values are stored in the database.

Domain object description. As discussed earlier, each domain object used in the system will have a corresponding description which will allow the object to be located and evaluated in an image. Each facial object (**face outline, nose, mouth, etc.**) can be described in this way. Consider the object **nose**. Since the **nose** object doesn't really correspond to a distinguishable region of the image, it is more effective to describe a **nose** based on the edges which represent the edges of the nose in the image. These are specified (rather simply) as two vertical edges, joined at the bottom by a horizontal edge. The most important information about this object is contained in the *occurrence* attributes:

Attribute	Value
Occurences per image	*Exactly 1*
Absolute location	*— no specification —*
Relative location	*Contained by* **face**
	Horizontally centered between **left_eye** *and* **right_eye**
	Vertically located between **left_eye** *and* **mouth**

Constraints describing the attribute variations such as scale, orientation, and angles are also defined. In the case of this object, variations in these attributes are minimal, since instances of this object will be very consistent in their size and orientation.

The above description is then used on the resulting data of the general segmentation. Since only vertical and horizontal edges are used in this description, only these are shown in the example. A graphical representation of this model is shown in figure 4, and two images representing the edges from the general segmentation are shown in figure 5. Although this is by no means the most powerful method for segmenting face images, it does have its benefits. Most importantly, it allows a user to define the objects he chooses without requiring specific vision routines to be written. It also provides a means to indicate which attributes of the object should be considered most important for similarity computations.

To locate this object, the set of edge elements in the description will be matched to the edge elements in the segmented edge image. The distances for

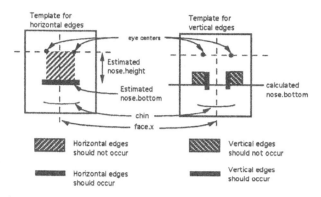

Fig. 4. Nose object description to be used with edge-images of figure 5.

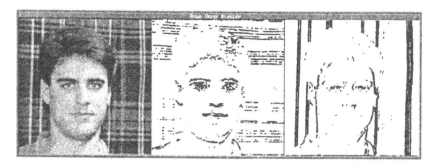

Fig. 5. a)Original face image b)Horizontal edge image c)Vertical edge image

the height and width of the nose will vary in order to maximize the matching of the template regions to the edge image. Since the **nose** will only be located once the **face**, **mouth** and the two **eye** objects have been located, inter-object relationships are used to supply a relative location for the **nose**. The bottom of the **nose** is known to exist between the horizontal centers of the eyes, and vertically between the eyes and the mouth. These relationships give an excellent approximation to the location of the nose in the image.

User-specified personnel data. In order to distinguish between different people in the database, identification attributes such as **name** and **social-security number** must be assigned to each face. However, there is no need to use only these basic attributes. Information such as age and sex can also be taken advantage of to improve the ability to retrieve the desired face, although this does avoid the basic problem we are addressing: *content-based* retrieval. However, this information fits very naturally into our interface. Since it is the user who actually guides the retrieval process, it is necessary to allow him to make use of this information if he chooses.

Derived feature values. The domain knowledge described above will provide the necessary data to locate and evaluate the necessary features of type $\mathbf{F}_d$. This is done feature-by-feature as determined by the ordering created in the domain object descriptions. For example, since the **nose** is dependent upon the location of the **face**, it will not be located until the **face** has been correctly segmented. In fact, the first feature to be found is the **face** object. Once this is located, objects such as the **eyes** and **nose** can also be segmented. This process is similar to that developed in [7] for locating facial features in images. Because of our domain, these types of relationships are very well-defined. This is important because the nature of our objects and features do not lend themselves well to very strict object models. Instead, we can use very non-restrictive models, but take advantage of the strong spatial constraints of the objects within the image. In fact it is necessary that we incorporate these spatial constraints into the object identification process. Without these constraints, many false occurrences of objects will be identified due to weak object models, shadows, etc.

Computable features. When an image is inserted into the system, each domain object $\mathbf{D}_j$ will be located, and the set of *derived* features, $\mathbf{F}_d$, of $\mathbf{D}_j$ will be calculated and stored. A subimage, $\mathbf{R}_j$ will also be stored for $\mathbf{D}_j$ (indirectly through IO_j) as described in section 5.2. This subimage will contain the segmented representation of $\mathbf{D}_j$ and is important for the efficient processing of *computable* features, $\mathbf{F}_c$. These types of features are necessary to avoid costly computations for features which are rarely required. For example, a blemish or scar on a person's face may be a very distinguishable feature. A user should be able to specify this type of feature when attempting to retrieve a specific face. However, it is not practical to examine every face for some type of irregular marking on any part of the face for two reasons. The first is that very few people will have such a feature. The process of finding such a marking will rarely provide additional information. Secondly, the required process is not very well-suited for the general case. That is, scars or other markings can come in many different forms, and it may be very difficult to distinguish between such a marking, and the effects of shadows, reflections, etc. This process is much more suited to examining a specific region of the face to determine if an irregular marking *could* be present. Thus, markings will be looked for only when and where a user specifies. It will be most efficient to do this process only on the candidate faces which satisfy the other criteria specified by the user. By maintaining this distinction between derived and computed features, additional features and relationships may be added as desired, without requiring the entire system or existing data to be altered. Thus, adding a feature f_a of type $\mathbf{F}_d$, does not require that all faces already in the database be re-processed to compute f_a. Instead, f_a can be computed as a derivable feature, $\mathbf{F}_d$, for new faces, and as a computable feature, $\mathbf{F}_c$, for faces already in the database.

8.2   Image Retrieval

When a user chooses to locate a specific face in the database, an interactive query process is initiated. The user is provided the option of specifying new descriptions of specific features, or iteratively altering the values for any of the features. Initially the user will describe the target person in terms of obvious attributes such as sex and age. The user may also specify other recognizable features, such as shade of the skin, and color of the hair, that will accurately describe the person. After the user has specified values for the desired features, the system will determine those faces in the database which are most similar to the described face. The determination of similarity values is a very subjective process, but will be based on the research discussed in [1, 6]. The **K** most similar faces (**K** = 3 in our initial implementation) will then be presented to the user for evaluation. The user may identify one of these faces as the chosen face, or choose to alter one of the faces to provide a more accurate description of his target face.

If the user chooses to alter one of these target faces, he must specify the individual facial features that should be altered. The alterations are processed with respect to the current values of the chosen face. In other words, the user does not specify a feature f_i (for example **color of hair**) to have a value V (for example, an RGB value), but rather that the value of the feature f_i is different (for example, **more blonde**) than its value in the displayed face. This allows the user to iteratively change those features which are different than those of the target face. When the user alters a feature f_i, he also specifies his confidence level in assigning this value. The value $Conf_i$ indicates how certain he is about the value assigned to f_i. It should be noted that the confidence values will not be made using numerical specifications. Instead, they will be chosen from a set of terms such as *very sure, somewhat sure,* and so on. This will provide a more consistent method of indicating certainty. When these alterations are specified, the database is again searched for those faces which are most similar to the face specified by the user. Note that features which were not chosen to be altered by the user, will retain the values of the features in the chosen displayed face. This process continues until the desired person has been located. Figure 6 shows the screen displaying the three most similar faces retrieved for a query. The top of the screen also shows the features for the object **hair** being altered for the next query. Along with each individual feature to be changed, the user indicates a degree of confidence in assigning a value to this attribute.

Initial feature specification. When a user begins a search for a face, characteristics such as **sex, age,** etc., will be specified, although any features may be used. All feature values specified by the user will be given an initial feature value based on the statistics for that feature. For example, if the user specifies the feature **nose.width**, f_i, to be **very wide**, the value for f_i in the target face will be assigned the value $\mu_{nose.width} + \text{vw}\sigma_{nose.width}$, where **vw** is a predefined

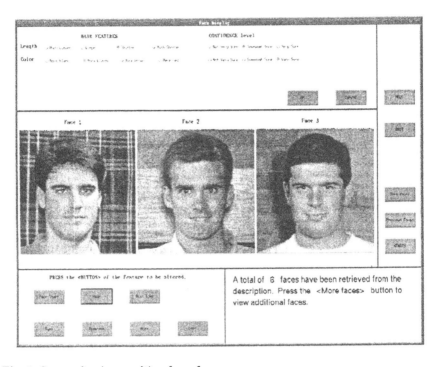

Fig. 6. Screen showing resulting faces from a query.

value corresponding to the user's choice **very wide**. These are the values that will then be used in the initial query.

Feature alteration. After this initial query is executed and the best fit faces are returned, the user may specify feature values based on one of the resulting faces. This allows the user to specify relative values such as **narrower**, **wider**, and **much wider** which is much more effective for describing a face than assigning actual values. It is also important to allow the user the ability to specify features using image-data, rather than textual descriptions or low-level image data, which is very complex and cumbersome. The new feature values of the target face T' are calculated as in section 6.2, and are defined as:

$$T'(i) = T(i) + \Delta_i * \sigma_i \quad \text{where}$$

$T(i)$ is the current value of feature f_i
$T'(i)$ is the resulting value of feature f_i
Δ_i is the *relative feature value change* which is defined below
σ_i is the standard deviation for f_i
Δ_i is the *relative feature value change* defined as:

$\Delta_i = \frac{\sigma_i \cdot K \cdot \delta_u}{N}$ where

σ_i is the standard deviation for f_i
K is the number of images to be retrieved
δ_u is the magnitude of the change specified by the user for *feature* f_i
N is the number of occurrences of f_i in the database

8.3 Image similarity

In order to determine the similarity between the user-described target image T, and a face F in the database, the distance between each of the individual features f_i is calculated as:

$$\delta(T, F, i) = \frac{|T(i) - F(i)|}{\sigma_i} C_i$$

where $T(i)$ *and* $F(i)$ are the actual data values and C_i is a constant used to scale the amount of deviation for different attributes.

Once these attribute differences are computed, the overall deviation between the images can be computed. This is calculated as:

$$\Delta(T, F) = \sum_i W_i Seg_i Conf_i \delta(T, F, i) \text{ where}$$

W_i is the *weight* of feature f_i
Seg_i is the *segmentation certainty* of feature f_i
$Conf_i$ is the *user's confidence* in describing f_i

The values $\Delta(T, F)$ are then used to determine the most similar faces to return to the user. Subsequent queries can then be specified using any of these returned images. This iterative process can continue until the desired image is retrieved.

9 Conclusion

We have presented a general system architecture which provides a framework for visual information management systems. Computer vision processes are integrated with standard information systems to make more effective use of the actual image data. These vision routines provide a very effective method of content-based querying which is lacking in many image-database systems. Our interactive retrieval process emphasizes QBE capabilities and allows complex image-based queries to be created very intuitively. These concepts have been implemented in a face image retrieval system, which allows a user to interactively describe a person using visual descriptions based on other face images, instead of strictly textual descriptions.

Acknowledgements

The authors would like to thank Imtiaz Ali, Allen Oh, and Deborah Swanberg for their efforts in the design and implementation of the face-image retrieval project.

References

1. V. Bruce, *Recognising Faces*, Lawrence Erlbaum Associates, Publishers, Hove and London, UK and Hillsdale, USA, 1988.
2. J. Cartoux, J. Lapreste, and M. Richetin, "Face authentification or recognition by profile extraction from range images," in *Proceedings of the Workshop on Interpretation of 3D Scenes*, pp. 194–199, Austin, TX, USA, November 1989, IEEE Computer Society Press.
3. V. Govindaraju, D. B. Sher, R. K. Srihari, and S. N. Srihari, "Locating human faces in newspaper photographs," in *Proceedings CVPR 1989*, pp. 549–554, San Diego, California, USA, June 1989, IEEE Computer Society, IEEE Computer Society Press.
4. A. Gupta, T. Weymouth, and R. Jain, "Semantic queries with pictures: the VIMSYS model," in *Proceedings of the 17th International Conference on Very Large Data Bases*, September 1991.
5. N. D. Haig, "Investigating face recognition with an image processing computer," in *Aspects of Face Processing*, H. D. Ellis, M. A. Jeeves, F. Newcombe, and A. Young, editors, pp. 410–425, Martinus Nijhoff Publishers, 1986.
6. L. D. Harmon, "The recognition of faces," *Scientific American*, pp. 71–82, October 1973.
7. T. Kanade, *Picture Processing System by Computer Complex and Recognition of Human Faces*, PhD thesis, Kyoto University, November 1973.
8. K. R. Laughery, C. Duval, and M. S. Wogalter, "Dynamics of facial recall," in *Aspects of Face Processing*, H. D. Ellis, M. A. Jeeves, F. Newcombe, and A. Young, editors, pp. 373–388, Martinus Nijhoff Publishers, 1986.
9. W. A. Phillipps and L. S. Smith, "Conventional and connectionist approaches to face processing by computer," in *Handbook of Research on Face Processing*, A. W. Young and H. D. Ellis, editors, pp. 513–18, Elsevier Science Publishers B.V., Amsterdam, The Netherlands, 1989.
10. J. Shepherd, "An interactive computer system for retrieving faces," in *Aspects of Face Processing*, H. D. Ellis, M. A. Jeeves, F. Newcombe, and A. Young, editors, pp. 398–409, Martinus Nijhoff Publishers, 1986.
11. T. J. Stonham, "Practical face recognition and verification with WISARD," in *Aspects of Face Processing*, H. D. Ellis, M. A. Jeeves, F. Newcombe, and A. Young, editors, pp. 426–441, Martinus Nijhoff Publishers, 1986.
12. K. Wong, H. H. Law, and P. W. M. Tsang, "A system for recognising human faces," in *Proceedings ICASSP 89*, pp. 1638–1642, May 1989.
13. C. J. Wu and J. S. Huang, "Human face profile recognition by computer," *Pattern Recognition*, vol. 23, no. 4, pp. 255–259, 1990.
14. A. W. Young and H. D. Ellis, editors, *Handbook of Research on Face Processing*, Elsevier Science Publishers B.V., Amsterdam, The Netherlands, 1989.

Queries in Object-Oriented Database Systems

Reda ALHAJJ   M.Erol ARKUN

Department of Computer Engineering
and Information Sciences
Bilkent University
Bilkent 06533, Ankara, TURKEY

Abstract

A query language is an important component of any database system. In object-oriented data models, although messages serve to manipulate the database, a query language is still required to effectively deal with more complex situations and to facilitate associative access. In this paper, a query language for object-oriented data models is described. It handles both the structure as well as the behavior of objects. Not only the manipulation of existing objects, but also the creation of new objects and the introduction of new relationships are supported by the language. Equivalents to the five basic operations of the relational model as well as other additional operations such as one level project and nest are defined. Both the operands as well as the results of these operations are characterized as having a pair of sets -a set of objects and a set of message expressions (sequences of messages) applicable to them. The closure property is shown to be preserved in a natural way by the results of operations possessing the same characteristics as the operands in a query. It is shown that every class possesses the properties of an operand by defining a set of objects and deriving a set of message expressions for it. It is also shown how the super\subclass relationships of the result of a query with its operands can be established and how the result can be placed persistently in the lattice as a class.

Keywords: *database system, object-oriented data model, object-oriented query language, object algebra, formal query model, algebraic operations.*

1 The Motivation and Related Work

Conventional data models are not considered powerful enough for engineering and scientific applications. Consequently, extensions to the relational model have been proposed [1, 19, 25, 33] and object-oriented concepts [23, 35] have been merged with database technology in developing object-oriented data models [13, 16, 21, 22, 24, 29, 30].

An object-oriented system is built using classes, objects, methods and messages. Classes are arranged in a hierarchy/lattice to overcome the redundancy and duplication in contents providing for reusability. Objects are considered as instances in classes for objects in the same class to share their common class facilities. Methods are included in classes to satisfy the encapsulation property. A method is invoked by an object when the latter receives the corresponding message. The behavior of objects in a class is represented by the set of methods of the class. The state of objects in a class is inferred from the common instance variables defined in the class.

Still there is no agreement on standardization within the realm of object-orientation. Neither the boundaries for the query model have been set up nor an object-oriented query language has been well defined yet. This is one of the common complaints against object-oriented databases [31].

Object-oriented databases support implicit queries for simple operations through messages, but a query language is required to be a part of any kind of database system. For instance, the message **name()** when sent to an object in a class, say *student,* the value of the **name** instance variable of the particular student object is returned. While a single message is sufficient for such an operation in the object-oriented context, a selection and a projection are necessary to get the same result in the relational model. An additional join should precede when **name** is not a column of the student relation. Another example can be seen in sending the message **courses()** to a student and the message **grade()** to the result obtained by the first message. Although it is handled due to the implicit join [27] present in object-oriented models, this corresponds to an explicit join in the relational model. The two messages **courses()** and **grade()** form a message expression. In general, a message expression is defined to be a sequence of messages $m_1...m_n$, with $n \geq 1$. Message expressions preserve encapsulation and information hiding.

While simple message expressions give superiority to object-oriented systems over the relational model, an *ad hoc* object-oriented query language is still needed for more complex situations and to support associative access. The relational model has superiority over the current object-oriented models as the achievement of the closure property is concerned. In an object-oriented model, it should be possible to use the result of a query operation as an operand.

Several query languages such as those of GemStone [29], O_2 [18], EXODUS [17], IRIS [22], ORION [14, 27], *OSAM** [2], Postgres [33], PDM [20, 30], EN-CORE [34, 39] and the formal calculi and algebra developed by Straube and T.

Özsu [37] in addition to others [3, 12, 32, 38] have been proposed. Some of these query languages are extensions to relational languages such as SQL and QUEL. While EXODUS and Postgres provide QUEL based query language, IRIS and O_2 provide an SQL like interface. In IRIS queries are translated into relational algebra expressions which are executed. Therefore the underlying query processor of IRIS is purely relational, and so IRIS violates the encapsulation principle.

Two trends are being followed in providing query support for object-oriented data models. In the first [2, 14, 17, 29, 37], only retrieval operations are supported while in the other [18, 20, 27, 30, 32, 34, 39] it is also possible to have operations that create new objects. The first group argue that there is no need to create new objects by introducing new relationships into the model as the required relationships are already defined at the modeling level. The proponents of the latter, that we agree with, argue that it is not possible to have all the required relationships defined at the modeling level. The need for new relationships arises later on trying to satisfy application requirements. So, the power of the model should not be restricted and the introduction of new relationships should be permitted.

A major drawback of the mentioned query languages is that when new objects are allowed in the result, the closure property is not properly satisfied. Nested relations [1, 25] are allowed as operands because the output of an operation is a nested relation. For instance, in O_2 values are introduced to maintain the closure property. The object algebra described in [34, 39] has its domain as sets of objects of the Tuple type in which nesting of tuples is possible and hence it is nothing more than the nested relational representation. We argue that nested relations do not form a proper logical representation of object associations.

In the query model of ORION [27], although the result of a query operation is a class, the improper placement of resulting classes in the lattice leads to duplication of class contents. Hence ORION violates the reusability feature of object-oriented systems. However, we argue that it is an overhead to have a class as the output of a query, except for permanent queries. In this paper we describe the output of a query by the minimum requirements of an operand, given next, and from such characteristics we can derive the characteristics of a class when persistency of the result is required. In $OSAM^*$ operands in a query are the database itself and all subdatabases derived from the original database by query operations; the result of a query is a subdatabase.

In this paper, we describe an object algebra for object-oriented databases. An operand has a pair of sets, a set of objects and a set of message expressions defined on elements of the first set. Also, the output of any operation has these two sets defined and derived from the sets of operand(s). By doing this, we are not violating any of object-oriented features in maintaining the closure property. Our object algebra is a superset of the relational algebra, but the semantics of the operations are different due to the object-oriented features. In addition to the relational operators, we define two other operators, nest and one level project. The nest operator serves to establish additional needed relationships that are not a priori defined in the model. It is an explicit join that serves the place of a missing implicit join. It is equivalent to the cross-product operation under certain conditions. The other operator, one level project, outputs the result of the evaluation of a set of message expressions against objects of the operand. The aim of this operator is to reduce the depth of nesting. So we have two different projection operators, the relational like projection operator does not evaluate any message expression but just serves to eliminate some parts of the structure. By using the operators of the algebra described in this paper, we will be able to manipulate existing objects and establish new relationships and hence new objects.

The rest of the paper is organized as follows. In section 2 we introduce the basic features of the data model on which the algebra is based. We define a set of objects for each class and show how a set of message expressions for a class can be derived. A class, having a set of objects and a set of message expressions, is shown to be an operand. The query language is described in section 3. A summary and conclusions are presented in section 4.

2   The Data Model

In this section, we describe the basic features of the data model on which the object-algebra is based. In our data model every item of the real world is represented as an object that captures both the state and behavior of the item. An object has an identity and a value. Identity distinguishes one object in the database from other existing objects and provides for object sharing [26]. A value may be either a single value or a set of values drawn from a domain. A domain is either atomic or non-atomic; an atomic domain may be any of the conventional domains including integers, characters, etc. On the other hand, a non-atomic domain includes the set of objects of a class as represented by their identities. The following are objects where o_i represents identity:

$o_1 <'' John'', 20 >$
$o_2 <'' Mary'', 19 >$
$o_3 <'' Jack'', 25, 5, \{o_6, o_7\} >$
$o_4 <'' Brown'', 40, 40K >$
$o_5 <'' Lee'', 22, 15K, 5, \{o_7\} >$
$o_6 <'' CS590'', 3 >$
$o_7 <'' CS565'', 4 >$

Related to an object we use value(o) and identity(o) to denote the value and the identity of object o, respectively. Unless confusion may arise, the identity function will be dropped and o will be used to represent identity(o).

Definition 2.1 (Equality of objects,) *Two objects o_1 and o_2 are:*
   - *identical ($o_1 = o_2$) iff identity(o_1)=identity(o_2)*
   - *shallow-equal ($o_1 \doteq o_2$) iff value(o_1)=value(o_2)*

- *deep-equal ($o_1 \hat{=} o_2$) iff by recursively replacing every object o_i in value(o_1) or value(o_2) by value(o_i), equal values are obtained.* □

$$(o_1 = o_2) \Rightarrow (o_1 \dot{=} o_2) \Rightarrow (o_1 \hat{=} o_2)$$
$$\text{identical} \Rightarrow \text{shallow-equal} \Rightarrow \text{deep-equal}$$

and these correspond to identity, shallow-equality and deep-equality of *Smalltalk-80* [23]. So, we have flexibility in comparing objects depending on these equalities.

Objects that have the same state structure are collected in one class. Looking at the previous objects, it seems that o_1 and o_2 should be in the same class. Inheritance is supported to overcome duplication and allow for reusability. Inheritance covers state structure and behavior. Next are the state structures of the classes related to the previous objects:

$person <\emptyset^*, name:string, age:integer >$
$student <\{person\}, year:integer, courses:course >$
$staff <\{person\}, salary:integer >$
$research\text{-}assistant < \{staff, student\} >$
$course <\emptyset, code:string, credit:integer >$

where any pair $iv : d$ represents an instance variable definition such that iv is the instance variable name and d is the underlying domain. For instance, age has an integer domain.

The first argument in a class definition is a set with elements being classes from which inheritance is achieved. We say that *person* is a superclass of *student* and *staff*, while each of *student* and *staff* is a subclass of *person*. Any instance in *student* or *staff* is actually an instance in *person* but the reverse is not true. This is because in general, a subclass may include additional instance-variables and behavior definition. As inheritance is concerned, classes are arranged in a lattice with the general class OBJECT at the root, i.e., a direct or indirect superclass of all other classes. We use $T_{instances}(c_i)$ to denote the set of total instances of class c_i:

$T_{instances}(person) = \{o_1, o_2, o_3, o_4, o_5\}$
$T_{instances}(staff) = \{o_4, o_5\}$
$T_{instances}(student) = \{o_3, o_5\}$
$T_{instances}(research\text{-}assistant) = \{o_5\}$
$T_{instances}(course) = \{o_6, o_7\}$

A class has a set of methods and for every method there is a corresponding message. A method implements a function and is invoked using a corresponding message. A method also has a number of arguments $n \geq 0$. We use messages(c) to denote the set of messages of the class c. Among the methods found in a class there exists a method corresponding to each of the instance variables of the class. The name of an instance variable when sent to an object as a message,

---

*$\emptyset$ indicates that there is no user defined superclass

returns the value of the instance variable in the receiving object. For instance, o_1 age() returns 20, while o_5 courses() returns $\{o_7\}$ and o_5 courses() code() returns $\{"CS565"\}$. Such methods return existing stored values while other methods that do not correspond to any instance variables return derived values, computed starting with existing stored values and possibly supplied parameters.

Definition 2.2 (Message expressions of a class)
Starting from the set of messages of a class c_i, messages(c_i), the set of possible message expressions of class c_i, denoted $M_e(c_i)$ can be recursively constructed by:

- *messages(c_i) is a subset of the set of message expressions of class c_i.*

- *if the domain of the result of a message expression $x_i \in M_e(c_i)$ is $T_{instances}(c_j)$ for some class c_j, then the concatenation of x_i m_j with $m_j \in messages(c_j)$ is an element of $M_e(c_i)$.* □

The two steps of definition 2.2 are used in deciding whether a given message expression is an element of $M_e(c)$ for a given class c.

3 The Object Algebra

In this section, we describe an object algebra where the closure property is maintained in a natural way without violating object-oriented features. Although most of the existing query languages are devoted to the manipulation of objects without creating new ones, we and others [32, 34, 39] argue the need for a more powerful query language that allows the creation of new objects in addition to the manipulation of existing ones. This adds the flexibility of introducing relationships into the model making the manipulation more powerful. An operand has a pair of sets, a set of objects and a set of message expressions. Since a class has a defined set of objects and a derived set of message expressions, a class can be used as an operand. The result of any query operation is also a pair of sets and may be made persistent in the lattice because it is possible to derive the state structure and behavior definition of the result of a query from those of the operand(s); hence it is a class [4].

Starting from a pair, a set of objects and a corresponding set of message expressions, it is possible to derive class characteristics, enumerated next. To recall, a class has a set of objects, a set of instance variables, a set of methods with corresponding messages in a one to one relationship, and a set of superclasses. A set of objects is given in the pair. So, finding a set of messages is equivalent to finding the set of methods and since an instance variable has a corresponding method, and hence a message, the set of instance variables is constructed by collecting those instance variables having a message in the calculated set of messages. The set of messages of a class is determined to include every message that appears as the first message in a sequence of messages that constitute an element of the set of message expressions of that class. Finally, the set of superclasses is determined according to the applied operation as indicated next in this section.

We differentiate between temporary and persistent evaluation of a query. An assignment free query is always evaluated on a temporary basis. The assignment symbol = is also used to denote such evaluation. The symbol := signifies the evaluation of a query on a persistent basis. While a temporary based evaluation of a query ends by finding only the pair of sets in the result, a persistent based evaluation continues with the finding of class characteristics of the determined pair. We manipulate objects depending on being identical, shallow-equal or deep-equal according to definition 2.1. The classes introduced in the previous section will be used in all the examples presented in this section. In the rest of this section, we assume A and B to denote either pairs like $<T_{instances}(A), M_e(A)>$ and $<T_{instances}(B), M_e(B)>$ or query expressions. A query expression is a sequence of one or more query operators applied to some operands to produce a pair of sets.

3.1 Selection

The selection operation presents a restriction on objects of the operand. In our object algebra, the selection has a single operand and produces an output that consists of a pair where the included objects are those satisfying a given predicate expression as defined next. The set of message expressions of the resulting pair is the same as that of the operand. The selection operation has the following definition:

$$\text{Select}(A, p) = < \{o \mid o \in T_{instances}(A) \land p(o)\}, M_e(A) >$$

where p is a predicate expression. In a predicate expression, one variable is bound to objects of the operand and other variables are constants or bound by other queries. Given an object o, we use $p(o)$ to denote the evaluation of predicate expression p by letting o substitute an object variable in p.

Definition 3.1 (A predicate expression)
The following are predicate expressions:

P1:   T and F are predicate expressions representing true and false.

P2:   Let y_1 and y_2 be two values with the same underlying domain such that at least y_1 or y_2 is of the form (o x), where o is an object variable bound to objects of an operand in a query and x is a message expression applicable to objects substituting o. Then:

[P2.1:] y_1 *op* y_2 *is a predicate expression where,*

$$op \in \begin{cases} \{=, \neq, \leq, \geq, >, <\} & \textit{if both } y_1 \textit{ and } y_2 \textit{ are single values from an} \\ & \quad \textit{atomic domain} \\[2ex] \{\in, \notin\} & \textit{if } y_1 \textit{ is a single value and } y_2 \textit{ is a set} \\ & \quad \textit{of values} \\[2ex] \{\subseteq, \not\subseteq, =, \neq\} & \textit{if both } y_1 \textit{ and } y_2 \textit{ are set of values, } y_2 \textit{ may be} \\ & \quad T_{instances}(e) \textit{ where } e \textit{ is a query expression} \\[2ex] \{=, \doteq, \cong\} & \textit{if both } y_1 \textit{ and } y_2 \textit{ are single values from} \\ & \quad \textit{a non-atomic domain, i.e., } T_{instances}(c) \\ & \quad \textit{for some class } c. \end{cases}$$

[P2.2:] $\forall | \exists z {\in} y_1 \wedge z$ *op* y_2 *is a predicate expression where,* y_1 *is a set of atomic or non-atomic values and*

$$op \in \begin{cases} \{=, \neq, \leq, \geq, >, <\} & \textit{if } y_2 \textit{ is a single value from an atomic domain} \\[2ex] \{\in, \notin\} & \textit{if } y_2 \textit{ is a set of values, } y_2 \textit{ may be } T_{instances}(e) \\ & \quad \textit{where } e \textit{ is a query expression} \\[2ex] \{=, \doteq, \cong\} & \textit{if } y_2 \textit{ is a single value from a non-atomic} \\ & \quad \textit{domain} \end{cases}$$

[P2.3:] $\exists z {\subseteq} y_1 \wedge z$ *op* y_2 *is a predicate expression where,* y_1 *is a set of values and*

$$op \in \begin{cases} \{\subseteq, \not\subseteq, =, \neq\} & \textit{if } y_2 \textit{ is a set of values, } y_2 \textit{ may be } T_{instances}(e) \\ & \quad \textit{where } e \textit{ is a query expression} \\[2ex] \{\ni, \not\ni\} & \textit{if } y_2 \textit{ is a single value} \end{cases}$$

P3:   *if p and q are predicate expressions then*   *(p),* $\neg p$, $p \wedge q$ *and* $p \vee q$ *are predicate expressions.*   □

Extending predicate expressions to allow quantifiers to permit the creation of objects does affect the query power. For example, $\exists x$, $x {\subseteq} T_{instances}(c)$ for some class c, binds x to a subset of $T_{instances}(c)$; objects in the subset to which x is bound could be built by this query. Such an object creation facility gives the algebra the power to do recursive queries by giving the ability to form a powerset [1]. Let s_1 and s_2 be object variables ranging over instances of the *student* class: $"CS590" \in s_1$ *courses() code()* is an example of P2.1 to check students attending "$CS590$"; $\exists c \in s_1$ courses() $\land$ $c \in s_2$ courses() $\land$ $s_1 \neq s_2$ is an example of P2.2 to check whether two given students have at least one course in common; $\forall c \in s_1$ courses() $\land$ $c \notin s_2$ courses() is an example of P2.2 to check whether two given students do not have any courses in common; $\exists c \subseteq s_1$ courses() $\land$ $c \subseteq s_2$ courses() is an example of P2.3 to check whether two given students have some courses in common.

Example 3.1: Find students attending CS590

$$S_1 = \text{Select}(student\%s, "CS590" \in s \text{ courses() code())}$$

where % indicates that the variable s is bound to and ranges over the objects of the operand, here the *student* class. More than one variable may range over objects of an operand. For example $student\%s_1\%s_2$ indicates that s_1 and s_2 range over objects of the *student* class. In the predicate expression, "$CS590$" $\in s$ courses() code(), the right hand side is of the form $(o\ x)$; hence satisfies definition 3.1. The use of "=" sign calls for an evaluation of this query on a temporary basis. Thus, the resulting pair S_1 consists of the sets $T_{instances}(S_1) = \{o_3\}$ and $M_e(S_1) = M_e(student)$. Notice that the student with object identity o_5 is not included in $T_{instances}(S_1)$ because of not attending the course "$CS590$".

Although Straube claims that a multiple operand selection is more powerful [37] than a single operand selection, we still insist on supporting the latter selection. Because Straube does not support the closure property in his algebra, he has the cross-product operation embedded into the selection. We argue that in comparing two algebras, the power of the whole algebra must be considered instead of the power of particular operations only. A language that supports the creation of new objects is necessary and considered more powerful than any other language devoted to the manipulation of existing objects only.

3.2 Project and One Level Project

The project operation serves to hide a subset of the message expressions of its operand without affecting the set of objects. Although the set of objects in a pair is in general heterogeneous, the only values accessed in each object are those specified by the set of message expressions of the pair. So, dropping some message expressions by the project operation hides the corresponding values in the accessible objects. The project operation is defined as follows:

$$\text{Project}(A, M_1) = <T_{instances}(A), M_1>$$

where $M_1 \subseteq M_e(A)$, i.e., an element of M_1 could be any message expression formed by definition 2.2. Only message expressions in M_1 can be applied to objects in the pair resulting from a project operation.

Example 3.2: Assume that the student class were not present in the lattice and the research-assistant class is defined as:

research_assistant<{*staff*},*year:integer,courses:course*>

To derive the student class as a persistent class and assuming that a student attends the department he works in, the research-assistant class is projected with respect to a set of messages:

student := Project(*research-assistant*, {*name(), age(), year(), courses()*})

The derived *student* class will be a direct superclass of the research-assistant class which is also modified as necessary. Not presented in this paper we derive algorithms to maximize reusability so that the derived *student* class will be recognized as a subclass of the person class and properly placed in the lattice on a persistent basis [4, 6].

Whereas the project operation merely associates the provided message expressions with the result without alteration, the one level project operation, defined next, computes a new set of objects and a corresponding set of message expressions. A specified subset of the message expressions of the operand is evaluated against objects of the operand to form new objects and a set of message expressions is formed to facilitate accessing the values encapsulated within the derived objects. The one level project has the following form:

$$\text{OLproject}(A,M_1) = < \{o \mid \exists o_1 \in T_{instances}(A) \wedge value(o) = (o_1 \ M_1)^{\dagger}\},$$
$$\{x \mid \exists x_1 \in M_1 \text{ with } x_1 \text{ returning a stored value, } x_1 = (x_2 \ m) \wedge$$
$$len(x_1) = len(x_2) + 1 \wedge \exists x_3 \in M_e(A) \wedge x_3 = (x_2 \ x) \wedge x = (m \ x_4)\}$$
$$\bigcup\{x \mid \exists x_1 \in M_1 \text{ with } x_1 \text{ returning a derived value, } len(x)=1 \wedge$$
$$\forall o_1 \in T_{instances}(A) \exists o \in T_{instances}(OLproject(A, M_1)) \text{ such that}$$
$$o_1 \ x_1 = o \ x\} >$$

where $M_1 \subseteq M_e(A)$. The one level project operation corresponds to a sequence of unnests followed by a projection in the nested relational model [1, 25].

OLproject(A,messages(A)$-\{m_1\}\bigcup(m_1$ messages(B))) unnests A with respect to B where $m_1 \in$ messages(A) and domain of m_1 is $T_{instances}(B)$. The depth of nesting decreases as the length of the longest message expression in M_1 increases. In other words, the depth of nesting is inversely proportional to the length of message expressions in M_1.

Example 3.3: *Find the names and course codes of students attending at least one course*

OLproject(Select(*student%s, s courses() ≠ ϕ*), { *name(), courses() code()*})

First students attending some courses are selected and the pair:

$< \{o_3, o_5\}, M_e(student) >$, i.e., all objects in $T_{instances}(student)$ are formed as an intermediate result. Second, the one level project operation is performed with the pair obtained by the selection operation as the operand to get the pair

$< \{< "Jack", \{"CS565", "CS590"\} >, < "Lee", \{"CS565"\} >\}, \{name(), code()\} >$

as the result.

$\dagger (o_1 \ M_1)$ returns the set of the results of the application of elements of M_1 to o_1.

The one level project operation does the function of project and image operations described in [34, 39] and the map operation described in [37], but we maintain the closure property without requiring additional constructs.

Concerning objects in the result of a one level project operation, deep-equal objects are automatically eliminated, i.e., no duplicates concerning deep equality are kept in the result. When required to be made persistent in the lattice, the result of the project operation is a superclass of the operand, whereas the result of the one level project operation is in general a direct subclass of the root, i.e., the OBJECT class.

Given a class c,   OLproject(c, messages(c))=Project(c, $M_e(c)$)=c.

3.3   Cross-product and Nest

Although many relationships between objects are represented by the interobject references built into the structure of the objects themselves, an explicit operation is still required to handle cases when a relationship is not present in the model. Both the cross-product and the nest operations are defined to introduce such relationships. While the cross-product operation is defined to be associative, the nest operation is not. However, the two operations are equivalent under certain conditions [7]. Associativity of the cross-product operation is useful in query optimization, although not discussed in this paper [4, 7]. A query expression is optimized after representing it by a binary tree with leaf nodes being operands as pairs and non-leaf nodes are operators of the object algebra.

Given two pairs A and B, their cross-product is defined by:

$$Cproduct(A,B)=<\{o|\exists o_1 \in T_{instances}(A) \exists o_2 \in T_{instances}(B)$$
$$\wedge\ value(o)=value(o_1).value(o_2)\},\quad M_e(A)\bigcup M_e(B)>$$

In this definition, we assume non-atomic underlying domains for all the instance variables of objects in A and B. Otherwise, i.e., having at least one underlying atomic domain, the definition is modified accordingly raising three other cases to consider. For objects of the pair that has at least one atomic underlying domain, the *value* function applied to the corresponding objects is replaced, in the above definition, by the *identity* function and the set of message expressions is preceded by a message m to reach the identities of the objects appearing as the argument of the *identity* function. Furthermore, $M_e(A)$ is replaced by $(m\ M_e(A))$ in the definition if the objects in A have at least one instance variable with an atomic underlying domain. By considering these four cases, the cross-product operation becomes associative [7].

When persistency is required in the lattice, the result of the cross-product operation is a subclass of the operand that has all non-atomic underlying domains and a direct subclass of the root otherwise.

The nest operation takes two operands and adds a value to each object in the first operand. Each such added value is the identity of the set of all objects in the second operand. Thus,

$$\text{Nest(A,B)}=<\{o \mid \exists o_1 \in T_{instances}(A) \exists o_2 \in T_{instances}(B) \wedge$$
$$value(o)=value(o_1).identity(o_2)\}, \quad M_e(A) \bigcup (m\ M_e(B))>$$

where the domain of m is objects in $T_{instances}(B)$. Notice that, Cproduct(A,B)= Nest(A,B) only when A has all non-atomic underlying domains, while B does not and Cproduct(A,B)=Nest(B,A) only when B has all non-atomic underlying domains while A does not.

The result of Nest(A,B), when required to be persistent is a subclass of A, i.e., the first operand.

Example 3.4: *Assume that both the student and the staff classes have an instance variable 'field' specifying the field of interest. To assign to every student the set of staff members that he can consult:*

$$\text{Nest}(student\%s_1, \text{Select(Difference}(staff, research\_assistant)\%s_2,$$
$$s_1\ field() = s_2\ field()))$$

notice that s_1 and s_2 are object variables bound to objects of the *student* class and the result of the difference operation, respectively. The difference operation is defined next in this section.

When combined with a selection operation, both of the cross-product and the nest operations result in a join operation. While the join due to a nest is an outer-join, the join due to a cross-product is an inner-join.

The Unnest(A,B) is an operation used to drop an existing relationship:

$$\text{Unnest(A,B)}=\text{Project}(A, M_e(A) - (m\ M_e(B)))$$

which projects on all message expressions of the operand A by eliminating the message expressions related to operand B. Here, $m \in messages(A)$ with domain $T_{instances}(B)$.

3.4 Set Operations

As mentioned before, the object algebra described in this paper handles and produces pairs of sets, a set of objects and a set of message expressions to handle the objects in the former set. Because we deal with sets, two basic set operations, union and difference, are supported by the object algebra; intersection is defined in terms of the difference operation.

The union operation returns a pair where the set of objects is in general heterogeneous and the set of message expressions is computed as the intersection of the sets of message expressions of the operands. A heterogeneous set of objects is the union of the sets of objects of the operands. The union operation is defined as follows:

$$\text{Union(A,B)}=<T_{instances}(A) \bigcup T_{instances}(B), \quad M_e(A) \bigcap M_e(B)>$$

In the resulting objects, only values of common instance variables and derived values are accessible, whereas the others are hidden because of the intersection of the message expressions of the operands.

When required to be persistent in the lattice, the resulting pair has the characteristics of a class which is a superclass of both operands.

Example 3.5: Assume that the person class were not present in the lattice with *student* and *staff* classes defined as follows:

$student<\emptyset, name{:}string, age{:}integer, year{:}integer, courses{:}course>$

$staff<\emptyset, name{:}string, age{:}integer, salary{:}integer>$

The person class is derived as:

$$person := Union(student, staff)$$

Concerning the difference operation, under the condition that $M_e(A) - M_e(B) \neq \phi$, the difference operation has the following form:

Difference(A,B)=$<\{o \mid o{\in}T_{instances}(A) \wedge o{\notin}T_{instances}(B)\}, \; M_e(A){-}M_e(B)>$

However, if it occurs that $M_e(A) - M_e(B) = \phi$, then $M_e(A) - M_e(B)$ is replaced by $M_e(A)$ in the definition.

Example 3.6: Find students who are not research assistants

Difference(*student, research-assistant*)

Since $M_e(student) \subseteq M_e(research\text{-}assistant)$, $M_e(student) - M_e(research\text{-}assistant) = \phi$ and in the output pair only $M_e(student)$ is returned according to definition 2.2.

Remembering that $T_{instances}(research\text{-}assistant) \subseteq T_{instances}(student)$, the same query can be coded using the select operation as follows:

Select(*student*%s, $s \notin T_{instances}(research\text{-}assistant)$)

Here s is bound to objects in the *student* class. Regardless of which one of the two forms is considered, the output pair of this query is $<\{o_5\}, M_e(student)>$.

When persistency is required, the result of a difference operation becomes a superclass of the first operand.

In terms of the difference we define the intersection operation as follows:

Intersection(A,B)=Difference(A,Difference(A,B))

4 Summary and Conclusions

In this paper we described queries in object-oriented data models. A query is coded using the operators of the object algebra applied on some operands. An operand should have a pair of sets, a set of objects and a set of message expressions. Elements of the latter set are used in the invocation of behavior as well as behavior constructors because a message expression leads to the execution of all the methods underlying the constituting messages and in the same order as if all together formed a single method. Concerning the result of a query, it is again a pair of sets, same as those of the operands. So, the output of one query can be the input of another without any problems and hence the closure property is maintained in a natural way. In producing the output pair of a query, the two constituent sets are derived in terms of those of the operand(s) and hence the operators act on the behavior as well as on the structure of objects. Behavior is necessary in maintaining the encapsulation feature of object-oriented data models. A query is handled on either a temporary or a persistent basis. Concerning the latter, for the output pair we derive the characteristics of a class and the inheritance relationship with other existing classes to properly place it in the lattice, thus achieving the benefit of reusability.

As a message expression may return computed in addition to stored values, the one level project operation of the object algebra is more powerful than the unnest operation of the nested relational model. This property is also valid for the object algebra as a whole, where computed as well as stored values may be manipulated.

Currently, we are examining the possibility of extending the algebra by adding new operations to improve its power. Also, the equivalence of different combinations of the operations are being tested for query optimization purposes.

References

1 S. Abiteboul, C. Beeri: "On the Power of Languages for the Manipulation of Complex Objects," INRIA, Tech.Rep.No. 846 (May 1988).

2 A. Alashqur, S. Su, H. Lam: "OQL: A Query Language for Manipulating Object-Oriented Databases," *Proceedings of the 15th International Conference on Very Large Databases*, Amsterdam (August 1989) 433–442.

3 A. Albano, L. Cardelli, R. Orsini: "Gelileo: A Strongly-Typed Interactive Conceptual Language," *ACM Transactions on Database Systems*, Vol. 10, No. 2 (1985) 230–260.

4 R. Alhajj (Al-Hajj): "A Query Model and a Query Language for Object-Oriented Database Systems," Technical Report, Bilkent University, Turkey (1991).

5 R. Alhajj (Al-Hajj), M.E. Arkun: "A Data Model for Object-Oriented Databases," *Proceedings of the 6th International Symposium on Computers and Information Sciences*, Antalya (October 1991).

6 R. Alhajj (Al-Hajj), M.E. Arkun: "A Formal Data Model and Object Algebra for Object-Oriented Databases," *Applied Mathematics and Computer Science*, Vol. 2, No. 1 (1992) 49-63.

7 R. Alhajj (Al-Hajj), M.E. Arkun: "A Query Language for Object-Oriented Databases," *Proceedings of the 7ᵗʰ International Symposium on Computers and Information Sciences,* Kemer-Antalya (November 1992).

8 R. Alhajj (Al-Hajj), M.E. Arkun: "Queries in Object-Oriented Database Systems," *Proceedings of the ISMM International Conference on Information and Knowledge Management,* Maryland (November 1992).

9 R. Alhajj (Al-Hajj), M.E. Arkun: "A Query Model for Object-Oriented Database Systems," *Proceedings of the 9ᵗʰ IEEE International Conference on Data Engineering,* Vienna (April 1993) (to appear).

10 R. Alhajj (Al-Hajj), M.E. Arkun: "Object-Oriented Query Language," *(Accepted paper) Journal of Information and Software Technology.*

11 R. Alhajj (Al-Hajj), M.E. Arkun: "An Object Algebra for Object-Oriented Database Systems," *(Accepted paper) Journal of ACM SIGBIT DATA BASE.*

12 F. Bancilhon, et.al.: "FAD: A Powerful and Simple Database Language," *Proceedings of the 13ᵗʰ International Conference on Very Large Databases,* Brighton (1987) 97–105.

13 J. Banerjee, et al.: "Data Model Issues for Object-Oriented Applications," *ACM Transactions on Office Information Systems,* Vol. 5, No. 1 (1987) 3–26.

14 J. Banerjee, W. Kim, K.C. Kim: "Queries in Object-Oriented Databases," *Proceedings of the 4ᵗʰ International Conference on Data Engineering,* Los Angeles, CA (February 1988) 31–38.

15 C. Beeri: "Formal Models for Object-Oriented Databases," *Proceedings of the 1ˢᵗ International Conference on Deductive and Object-Oriented Databases* (December 1989) 370–395.

16 M.J. Carey, D.J. Dewitt: "The Architecture of the EXODUS Extensible DBMS," *Proceedings of the IEEE International Workshop on Object-Oriented Database Systems,* Pacific Grove, CA (September 1986) 52–65.

17 M.J. Carey, D.J. DeWitt, S.L. Vandenberg: "A Data Model and a Query Language for EXODUS," *Proceedings of ACM-SIGMOD Conference on Management of Data,* Chicago (May 1988) 413–423.

18 S. Cluet, et al.: "Reloop, an Algebra Based Query Language for an Object-Oriented Database System," *Proceedings of the First International Conference on Object-Oriented and Deductive Databases* (December 1989).

19 C.J. Date: *An Introduction to Database Systems,* 4ᵗʰ Edition, Vol. 1 and Vol. 2, Addison-Wesley (1986).

20 U. Dayal: "Queries and Views in an Object-Oriented Data Model," *Proceedings of the Second International Workshop on Database Programming Languages* (June 1989) 80–102.

21 O. Deux, et al.: "The Story of O2," *IEEE Transactions on Knowledge and Data Engineering*, Vol. 2, No. 1 (1990) 91–108.

22 D.H. Fishman, et al.: "IRIS: An Object-Oriented Database Management System," *ACM Transactions on Office Information Systems*, Vol. 5, No. 1 (1987) 48–69.

23 A. Goldberg, D. Robson: *Smalltalk-80: The Language and Its Implementation*, Addison Wesley (1983).

24 M.F. Hornick, S.B. Zdonik: "A Shared Segmented Memory System for an Object-Oriented Database," *ACM Transactions on Office Information Systems*, Vol. 5, No. 1 (1987) 70–95.

25 G. Jaeschke, H.J. Schek: "Remarks on the Algebra of Non-First Normal Form Relations," *Proceedings of the Symposium on Principles of Database Systems*, (March 1982) 127–138.

26 S.N. Khoshafian, G.P. Copeland: "Object Identity," *Proceedings of the International Conference on Object-Oriented Programming Systems, Languages and Applications*, Portland, OR (September 1986) 406–416.

27 W. Kim: "A Model of Queries for Object-Oriented Databases," *Proceedings of the 15th International Conference on Very Large Databases*, Amsterdam (1989) 423–432.

28 W. Kim: "Object-Oriented Databases: Definition and Research Directions," *IEEE Transactions on Knowledge and Data Engineering*, Vol. 2, No. 3 (1990) 327–341.

29 D. Maier, J. Stein: "Development and Implementation of an Object-Oriented DBMS," In: Shriver B. and P. Wegner (eds): Research Directions in Object-Oriented Programming, MIT Press, Cambridge, MA (1987).

30 F. Manola, U. Dayal: "PDM: an Object-Oriented Data Model," *Proceedings of the International Workshop on Object-Oriented Databases*, Pacific Grove, CA (1986) 18–25.

31 E. Neuhold, M. Stonebraker: "Future Directions in DBMS Research," Technical Report 88-001, Intl. Computer Science Inst., Berkeley, CA (May 1988).

32 S.L. Osborn: "Identity Equality and Query Optimization," *Proceedings of the 2nd International Workshop on Object-Oriented Database Systems*, Ebernburg (September 1988) 346–351.

33 L.A. Rowe, M. Stonebraker: "The Postgres Data Model," *Proceedings of the* 13th *International Conference on Very Large Databases,* Brighton (1987) 83–96.

34 G. Shaw, S.B. Zdonik: "A Query Algebra for Object-Oriented Databases," *Proceedings of the* 6th *International Conference on Data Engineering,* Los Angeles, CA (1990) 154–162.

35 M. Stefik, D.G. Bobrow: "Object-Oriented Programming: Themes and Variations," *AI Magazine,* (January 1986) 40–62.

36 M. Stonebraker, et.al.: "Third Generation on Database System Manifesto," *Proceedings of IFIP DS-4 Workshop on Object-Oriented Databases* (1990).

37 D. D. Straube, M.T. Özsu: "Queries and Query Processing in Object-Oriented Database Systems," *ACM Transactions on Information Systems,* Vol. 8, No. 4 (1990) 387–430.

38 C. Zaniolo: "The Database Language GEM," *Proceedings of ACM-SIGMOD Conference on Management of Data,* San Jose, CA (May 1983) 207–218.

39 S.B. Zdonik: "Data Abstraction and Query Optimization," *Proceedings of the* 2nd *Workshop on Object-Oriented Database Systems,* Ebernburg (September 1988) 368–373.

Consistency Checking in Object Oriented Databases: a Behavioral Approach

Herve Martin[1], Michel Adiba[1], Bruno Defude[2]

[1] Laboratoire de Génie Informatique, IMAG-Campus,
BP 53X 38041 Grenoble Cedex, France
[2] Institut National des Télécommunications, 9, Rue Charles Fourier,
91011 Evry Cedex, France

Abstract. This paper presents a mechanism to enforce consistency in object oriented DBMS using pre-conditions and post-conditions on methods. This mechanism is coupled with an exception mechanism to allow deferred controls and semantic tolerance. Conditions are defined using SQL-like expressions and methods composition. A prototype which has been implemented on the O2 object oriented database management system (DBMS) is also described in this paper.

1 Introduction

Computer-aided design (CAD) and software engineering require the development of large-scale applications managing large amounts of persistent and shared data. Powerful constructors for data modeling are needed to meet the requirements of schema design. So, extensions of existing models or definitions of new ones (semantic data models, functional data models, object oriented data models [5]) have been proposed. The object oriented approach is going to influence future application development. Several projects are currently underway for the development of object oriented DBMS (Object-Store, Gemstone, O2, Ontos [2][5]).

Modelling behavioral aspects of objects is the basis of the object oriented approach [9]. However, we claim that these aspects need further developments especially in the framework of object oriented DBMS which are now emerging. In such a framework, our objective is to adopt a behavioral point of view for expressing database consistency.

In relational systems, data consistency is expressed by a set of integrity constraints, which captures the consistent states of the database. Commercially available systems are very poor for providing integrity control because static control increases significantly the execution time. Several projects addressing new applications such as CAD [4] tried to transpose integrity control from relational systems to object oriented ones. We think that this resulted in a static approach which sometimes needs human interaction and, therefore, cannot be general.

On the contrary, our proposals are not too far from programming languages pre-condition and post-condition mechanisms. Nevertheless, they are not based upon the Hoare logic [15], because of the specificity of the database area. One of our main ideas is to associate pre-conditions and post-conditions to methods. Methods are used to define object behavior. Then, by associating conditions to them, we can control that a given object will have a consistent behavior. In databases, the transaction concept allows an object to be temporarily inconsistent, so we introduce an exception mechanism to overcome this problem. Moreover, the language used to specify integrity constraints is a high level language using SQL-like expressions.

A prototype has been developed with the object oriented DBMS O2 [10]. However, our propositions can be easily adapted to other object oriented DBMS that use concepts defined in [2].

The remainder of the paper is organized in the following manner. Section 2 surveys related work on data integrity in the area of programming languages and database systems. Section 3 details our approach. Section 4 presents the implementation of our integrity control mechanism in the object oriented DBMS O2. Section 5 contains our conclusions and perspectives.

2 Related Work

To insure object oriented database integrity we were influenced by works in the area of DBMS, but also in the area of software engineering. These two domains share the same kinds of problems: to formally specify consistency and to propose a checking mechanism. Both in database and software engineering, works on formalisms to express integrity have been strongly influenced by logic. In the DBMS approach, integrity is expressed by a set of predicates, called integrity constraints, that must hold on each database state (at the end of a transaction). The DBMS is responsible for enforcing them, but controls can be statically performed. We name this approach: the static one. In the case of software engineering, the execution of an operation is submitted to the evaluation of a predicate, called a precondition. So, the evaluation of consistency is established at the operation level. We call this kind of approach: the dynamic approach.

2.1 The Static Approach

Almost all database systems of integrity control are based on a static approach. The execution of a program that includes database operations is called a transaction. There are several properties that transactions should have. The following are the main desirable properties (ACID):

1. **Atomicity**: A transaction is an atomic unit of processing; it is either performed entirely or not at all.
2. **Consistency**: A correct execution of the transaction must transform the database from one consistent state to an other one.
3. **Isolation**: A transaction should not make its updates visible to other transactions until it is committed.
4. **Durability**: The effect of all operations of the transaction is recorded permanently in the database.

It is the responsibility of the recovery system to insure atomicity and durability. Consistency is the most interesting aspects for us. To capture consistent states of the database, the user defines a set of integrity constraints. An integrity constraint is a logical expression on the value of some attributes or on some aggregates. In this context, we have to accept some inconsistent states during transaction execution. So, there are two points where integrity controls should be made: at the beginning of the transaction (to ensure that the database is in a consistent state) and at the end (to ensure that the transaction returns the database to a consistent state) (see Fig. 1). In general, it is enough to control the database state at the end of the transaction, because one can always assume that, before starting a new transaction, the resulting state of the previous one was consistent. The main advantage of the integrity constraint approach is its

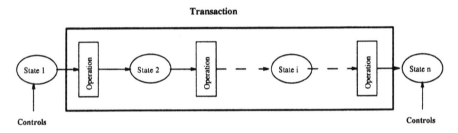

Fig. 1. Observable points in a transaction

high degree of semantic. The database semantic is clearly defined within general assertions, which allow a global view of integrity to be kept. Integrity constraints can be considered as a set of assertions expressed in a first order language. Thus, it is possible to combine or to decompose some assertions. In this approach, consistency is seen as logical properties on the different objects of the database. Moreover, the specification language is generally a declarative and powerful one based on a SQL-like syntax that offers many capabilities.

The main drawbacks of this approach are the following. First, only static constraints can be formally expressed, although sometimes it is necessary to refer to old and new database values. Moreover, it should be useful to associate constraints to specific update operations. Works on INGRES (query rewrite) [20] and in [19], and now on POSTGRES (a general rule mechanism) [5], are examples of the necessary extensions for handling dynamic aspects. The performance issue is the second main drawback of the static approach. In theory, at the end of a transaction, all constraints have to be evaluated on every object of the database. In reality, even though some optimizations have been proposed, this solution does not seem very realistic.

2.2   The Dynamic Approach

Previous works tried to solve the consistency problem by using a dynamic approach which makes reference to operations. The main attempts are those proposed in active databases, based on a trigger mechanism, and those that can be found in software engineering, especially in object oriented languages and interconnection models.

Active databases capture dynamic aspects with triggers under the form of event-condition-action rules [8][7][6][12]. When a significant event arises, the associated condition is evaluated and, if the result of the evaluation is positive, a specific action is executed. This mechanism is powerful, because the user defines not only the rules to evaluate but also when the evaluation has to be done. However, this approach has a main disadvantage because it is almost impossible to avoid side effects coming from the execution of the triggerred actions. The possibility of associating actions in case of violation of a rule is difficult to maintain because of side effects.

Our approach relies mostly on object oriented languages like Eiffel [18] or Smalltalk [14]. Even though the consistency checking problem is quite different, especially concerning the set and the transaction concepts, some techniques used to check the correctness of methods and enforce the extensibility and reusability of programs might be used in object oriented databases environment.

For example, in Eiffel a mechanism of pre-condition and post-condition based on the Hoare logic is proposed. There are three kinds of assertions: pre-conditions, post-conditions and invariants. If the pre-condition is true, it is possible to ensure that the post-condition will be reached and the invariant still holds.

Before any method execution (routine in Eiffel), the associated pre-condition is checked; after method execution post-conditions are checked. Invariants have to be always satisfied by any objects of the class.

Interconnection models are an extension of the Hoare logic. These models are used to manage the evolution of large softwares. They allow the modeling of links between different software components. For example, the Inscape project [11], is an extension to the concept of post-condition: with post-conditions, it is possible to control the side effects of an operation. In this model, the specification of exceptions is another extension to the Hoare logic. Exceptions allow for definition of the correct behavior in case of pre-condition violation.

In these approaches, the level of specification is quite low (e.g. it concerns opening or closing files), but it is a good example of property specifications linked to consistency of operations.

In a dynamic approach, consistency is treated at the operation level: the precondition mechanism in software engineering and in programming languages, triggers in active databases. There are numerous advantages to this approach. The modeling capability is increased. It is possible to define condition both on operations and on related objects. Controls can be computed in a reasonable time execution, because the checking mechanism knows on what object the control operates and when to make this control. The major drawback of this approach is its lack of clarity compared to the static approach. The specifications are split in the different operations, and the global view of consistency is lost.

Nevertheless, the dynamic approach seems to be a good one in many ways and might be interesting in an object oriented context. We now present our approach, which takes into account some concepts derived from the dynamic approach.

3 The Behavioral Approach

In our study, we found that the concept of transactions applied to object oriented databases needs more clarification. In most of the object oriented DBMS that we studied a transaction is merely a set of actions, but with very poor semantic considerations. In order to be general enough, we consider that a transaction in the object oriented DBMS world consists of messages sent to (database) objects. This corresponds, for instance, to an application program in O2. Of course, such transactions should have the ACID properties (section 2.1), but these properties should be re-interpreted in object oriented terms. We consider also that a transaction can include interactions through a human interface and be executed in the framework of new applications [3].

3.1 Consistent Object Behavior

Traditionally, each object has an identifier and encapsulates a (complex) value. Encapsulation insures that the behavior of each object type is defined by a set of methods. These methods are related either to the correponding object class (some of them can be inherited from super classes) or attached to the object itself (considered in some systems as a first class citizen). We associate the notion of consistency not on the object value but on the behavior of the object with respect to the way it is going to receive and answer messages.

During transaction execution, each object should behave correctly with respect to the specific context of this particular execution. This means that before answering a message, it should be possible to check whether specific preconditions hold. If not, the object will reject the message, and this will result in the transaction abortion. We say that the execution context (or "in_context" in our terminology) is not safe for a consistent execution of the corresponding method. The pre-conditions are expressed at the outside of the body of a given method, using a declarative language. In our approach this will generate automatically the necessary code for a specific system , in our prototype CO2 code.

If the pre-condition holds, the method is executed but still in the transaction framework. By using post-conditions, it is therefore possible to check if this execution resulted in a consistent behavior. A very flexible mechanism is defined which provides either transaction abortion or an exception raise. In the later case, exceptions are processed at the end of the transaction, before commit.

The main idea of our approach is to use the concept of behavior to ensure database consistency. Instead of constraining object states, we constrain their behavior. We consider that, if the behavior of objects is consistent during a transaction, then the transaction will keep the database in a consistent state. On the contrary, if the object behavior is detected as an inconsistent one, it is possible to eliminate this inconsistency or to signal it to the user.

Of course, defining such constraints as pre- or post- conditions is a matter of object modeling. We think that our proposition is general enough for dealing with different kinds of consistency problems. For example, to define range constraints on the salary of an employee, we express a behavioral constraint on the method update_salary as follows (the syntax will be described later, but is almost self explanatory):

Example 1 (Range constraint).

add method Update_salary (new_sal:FLOAT) **in class EMPLOYEE** **in_context** {new_sal > 1000}

Our approach is based on the assumption that a sequential composition of locally consistent behavior, gives as result a globally consistent behavior. To check consistency using the behavioral approach, we allow the user to specify controls at two levels: at the method execution level (local level) and at the transaction level (global level).

Controls at the local level can be done upon the reception of the message (before the beginning of the execution) or after the execution. Checks before the execution are used to verify the consistency of the execution context for the method. These checks are mainly based on the value of the parameters and/or on the state of the object that has received the message. Controls after method execution are used to check the validity of the behavior and are mainly based on the result of the method and/or the state of the object(s) after method execution.

This definition of consistency is very strong and must be relaxed to take into account two problems. First, some behaviors cannot be characterized locally but only globally at the end of the transaction. These kinds of behaviors must be considered to be suspicious at the local level and must be globally evaluated at the end of the transaction when all the required information is available. According to the context, we take the decision of accepting or refusing the behavior at the global level. If one of the suspicious behaviors is judged as inconsistent, the transaction will be aborted. Secondly, as was said above, a consistency mechanism must be flexible enough to take into account exceptions to the general rules. So before refusing a behavior, we need to check whether the present case refers to an exceptional case. Exceptional cases must be considered as correct and not as inconsistent.

To define checks at local and global levels, we propose two mechanisms. The first one is based on the activation context of a method (in_context), and the second one is based on the validation context of a method (out_context). The out_context is used to specify controls after the method execution and controls at the end of the transaction. It is associated with an exception mechanism.

Transaction

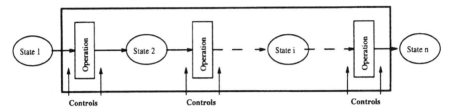

Fig. 2. Control points

Figure 2 shows the execution principle of a transaction with the different controls. As can be seen in this schema, all controls can generate an interruption of the transaction.

3.2 Activation Context

A pre-condition defined by the in_context clause concerns mainly the receiver state. It can be used also to check objects which are related to the receiver by the composition links or to verify the parameters of the message. The in_context clause is part of the method signature and its general syntax is the following:

add method method_name (param_list): type_of_result **in class** class_name
in_context {condition_of_activation}

A complete description of the language for expressing the conditions can be found in [17]. Here, we give only its main characteristics through several examples. We use a functional notation for methods invocation. For example m(x,p1,p2) expresses the activation of method m on object x with parameters p1 and p2. The receiver object is denoted by the keyword RECEIVER. This language provides control on:

1. the state of the receiver object,
2. the parameters of the message,
3. the objects linked to the receiver,
4. the state of a set of objects.

Our language allows one to express controls such as constraints on set cardinality or on aggregates (minimum, maximum, average), or to specify properties on sets (with a select - from - where notation).

Assume that a database schema consists of two classes EMPLOYEE and DEPARTMENT. An object of the class EMPLOYEE has several methods. For example, the method Address that gives an employee's address, the method Age that gives an employee's age, the method Salary that gives an employee's salary and the method The_department that returns the employee's department. The DEPARTMENT class has such methods as Manager that returns the EM-PLOYEE instance which is the manager of the department and Dname that returns a string representing the department name. Note that in our approach, we do not speak about attributes. For us an attribute takes place in the implementation part of the class and we only address the methods of the class.

For example, to specify a range constraint on the salary of an employee, we define a pre-condition on the method Update_salary:

Example 2 (Range constraint on the salary of an employee).

add method Update_salary (new_sal:FLOAT) **in class** EMPLOYEE
in_context {new_sal > Salary (RECEIVER)}

This pre-condition expresses that the salary of an employee can not decrease. Moreover, if it is forbidden for an employee to earn more that his/her manager, we write:

Example 3 (An employee earns less that his/her manager).

add method Update_salary (new_sal:FLOAT) **in class** EMPLOYEE
in_context {new_sal > Salary (RECEIVER) and new_sal < Salary (Manager (The_department (RECEIVER)))}

3.3 Validation Context

As was said before, the validation context (**out_context** clause) is used to specify controls after the method execution and at the end of the transaction. Both possibilities should be considered. The validation context is associated with an exception mechanism. According to the behavioral approach, controls that are specified in the **out_context**, meet two requirements.

First, they can detect **abnormal** behaviors which occur during method execution. The abnormal behaviors are special conditions that could not have been detected before execution (i.e. using the **in_context** clause) and that are unacceptable. They correspond to the effects of the methods on the current database objects. By providing actions, such unacceptable behavior can be eliminated.

Second, they can detect **suspicious** behaviors. By this we mean special conditions that cannot be considered as errors, but which can eventually be treated as temporary inconsistencies. When such a case is encountered, our mechanism will register it, and the final decision will be postponed until the end of the transaction. This approach can be used to treat semantic tolerance as defined in [13].

Exception Mechanism. Each time we detect either a suspicious or an abnormal behavior, an exception is raised. Each exception has a name and can have some parameters associated with it. A routine is associated with a given exception. There are two kinds of exceptions: IMMEDIATE or DEFERRED.

If the exception type is IMMEDIATE, then the exception manager calls the special routine associated to the exception raised. This routine either allows transaction execution to resume or triggers an abort.

If the type of the exception is DEFERRED, then the exception manager stores the exception in a set of "pending exceptions" together with its parameters. These parameters represent the exception context and will be used at the end of the transaction when executing the corresponding routine. Afterwards, a message *continue* is sent to the transaction.

At the end of the transaction, a message *end_of_transaction* is sent to the transaction manager. At this time, the transaction manager calls every exception routine that is pending. If all routines return a continue message, then the transaction commits, otherwise it aborts.

The Out-context Clause. The **out-context** clause is also part of the method signature. So, the syntax of a method definition becomes:

add method Method_name (param_list): type_of_result **in class** class_name
in_context {condition_of_activation}
out_context
{**when** <condition> **signal** <exception>(<param_list>)
...
when <condition> **signal** <exception>(<param_list>)}

In an **out_context** condition, it is also possible to use the keyword RECEIVER (as in the in_context clause). The keyword RESULT denotes the object returned as result if any.

Exception definition is also made at the schema definition level. An exception has a name, some parameters, a type (IMMEDIATE or DEFERRED) and a list of conditions with associated actions. The syntax is as follows:

define exception <name>(<parameter_list>) **of type** <exception_type>
{<condition> : <action>;
...
<condition> : <action>}

with:

<exception_type> ::= DEFERRED | IMMEDIATE
<action> ::= REFUSE | ACCEPT
<condition> ::= <user_defined_condition> | SAME

The definition of some conditions at the exception definition level is used firstly to refine the condition that has been defined at the method level and secondly to take into account exceptional behavior. It also permits reduction of the number of exceptions. The keyword SAME means that the condition is the same as the one defined in the out_context.

To avoid side effects and multiple exception triggering, only two actions associated with exceptions are allowed: REFUSE or ACCEPT.

An Example. As an example, we consider a simple application for student registration. We consider a set of students and two operations related to student registration to some modules. "Search-student(num:integer):STUDENT" looks in the database to determinate whether a student having num as number exists. If yes, it returns the corresponding instance, and if not, it raises an exception. The method Registration() can be used to register an existing student, according to specific rules. Each student should take at least 6 modules, but he/she can have a credit for at most one module. The modules are either mandatory or optional, but the choice of a student should include at least some mandatory modules which depend on the student profile. *Example 4* (signal student not found).

add method Search-student (number:integer):STUDENT **in class** STUDENT
out_context
{**when** RESULT = nil **signal** not_found}

The keyword RESULT refers to the STUDENT instance which is the result of the method. If there is no student corresponding to the given number, then the exception is raised. The definition of this exception is:

define exception not_found **of type** IMMEDIATE
{SAME : REFUSE}

This exception is very simple, we chose here to abort the transaction into which such a method will be called. Of course, there are other ways to write this method, depending on the semantic of the application.

Example 5 (Validate the registration).

Validation of each student registration means that we want to check whether the total number of taken modules is correct and, also, to check whether the choosen modules are consistent with respect to the rule about mandatory and optional modules.

add method Registration **in class** STUDENT
out_context
{**when** Nb_module (RECEIVER) < 6 **signal** pb_of_hours (RECEIVER)
when true **signal** mandatory_check (RECEIVER)}

define exception pb_of_hours (e:STUDENT) **of type** DEFERRED
{nb_course (e) < 5 : REFUSE;

nb_course (e) >= 6 : ACCEPT ;
nb_course (e) = 5 and credit (e) = 1 : ACCEPT ;
nb_course (e) = 5 and not (credit (e) =1) : REFUSE}

This exception will be processed at the end of the transaction (because its type is DEFERRED). The control could not have been done immediately because of the lack of information about student registration at that time.

define exception mandatory_check (e:STUDENT) **of type** DEFERRED
{ NOT (ALL &C
          IN   SELECT Mandatory(&p)
                FROM DEGREES &p
                WHERE &p = Degree(e)
          ENFORCE &C IN Modules(e)) : REFUSE}

This exception checks that a student is registered in all the mandatory courses of his/her degree. This exception is always raised by the method Registration. The associated treatment is expressed in a set-oriented way. All the mandatory courses &C of the degree &p corresponding to the student e must be among the chosen courses of this student e.

4 Implementation

An implementation of our proposals has been done on top of the object oriented DBMS O2 [10][16]. The O2 data model relies on two kinds of concepts: values and objects. An object consists of a pair (identifier, value), on which a predefined set of methods is defined. Definitions of objects with the same structure and the same behavior are grouped into the same class. Classes are connected by inheritance links that allow incremental specification. Methods are associated to classes and define the behavior of class instances. Finally, an application program includes database access operations and method calls. In our implementation, an application program is equivalent to a transaction.

As we explained before, we have extended the definitions of an O2 schema by adding consistency specifications in the signature of a method. We have adopted a generation approach which means that we have developed a specific generator, which takes as input methods signatures including in_context and out_context clauses and which generates appropriate CO2 code. Then, this code runs directly under the control of the O2 run time system. From the user point of view, this means that when the programmer writes a method, he can "extract" from his code specific instructions used for consistency checking. These instructions are expressed using our language, which results in more readable source code, and, in this way, different consistency control policies can be implemented. Moreover, this generator approach has several other advantages:

1. **Independence**: we use the O2 DBMS to implement our propositions, but without many changes, it is possible to implement it on another object oriented DBMS.

2. **Productivity**: This approach improves productivity of the developer by reducing the amount of code to write in methods.

3. **Reusability**: We can easily imagine that if we add specifications to methods, we improve their readability and their reusability.

4. **Extensibility**: It is easy to add new tools without any effects on present specifications.

5. **Implementation** facilities: Using tools under UNIX, results on the O2 DBMS can be tested quickly.

6. **Performance**: Our generation approach leads to code which is executed as part of a method. In this way, at execution time, there is no overhead from the system to control consistency aspects.

Figure 3 shows a simplified description of the generation process. From in_context, out_context and exception declarations, classes and methods dedicated to consistency checking are generated.

The problem of the generation, is to generate the whole of the checking mechanism in terms of O2 concepts: objects, methods and classes. From the checking mechanism point of view, we are concerned with different concepts: pre-conditions, post-conditions, exceptions and transactions. The main problem is to take into account the transaction concept (application in the O2 prototype that we have used) in order to allow asynchronous controls.

The in_context transformation is quite simple, because the in_context just consists of the specification of controls to perform immediately when the method is activated. So, we generate a method and the instruction which corresponds to its call. The generated method contains the result code of the interpretation of our language into CO2 language. Because CO2 is a DataBase Programming Language (DBPL), it was not very difficult to write the grammar corresponding to the transformation.

For the out_context and exception transformation, we have used the class and object concepts. We first generate a superclass called EXCEPTION. Each time a new exception is defined, a new class which inherits from the class EXCEPTION is created. This class has the attributes corresponding to the context of the exception. For example, if an exception E1 is defined with two parameters P1 of class C1 and P2 of class C2, then we generate a class E1 with two attributes P1 and P2. Attached to the exception class (as E1) are the methods allowed to affect the attributes of an object of the class and the method corresponding to the CO2 code generated from the condition definition. The metaclass EXCEPTION contains the definition of methods for the manipulation (creation and deletion) of exception objects.

When an exception is raised, an object of the corresponding class exception is created. If the type of the exception is immediate, the associated method is performed. Otherwise, the exception object is stored into the exception class. Now, we present the different steps of the generation process. Except steps 1 and 2, the compilation is the same as the usual one in O2. In the generator, the **in_context** generation consists of three steps.

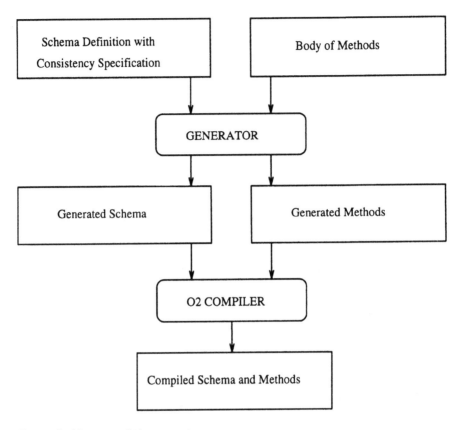

Fig. 3. Architecture of the generator

1. The first step is the definition of a method with name in_M, where M is the name of the method with the constraint. This method has the same parameters as the method M and is defined on the same class. The result of this method is an object of type boolean .

2. The second step is the generation of the body of the method in_M. This body is the result of the translation of the declarative expression of condition to the CO2 language, used by the O2 DBMS.

3. The third step is the incorporation of a call to in_M into the body of M. We generate also a conditional statement to check the result of in_M. If the result is false, we stop the execution and we print a report to the user.

Treating the **out_context** clause is a little bit more complicated, because of exceptions. The different steps are:

1. We begin by generating different classes that are necessary for taking exceptions into account. We generate a class EXCEPTION and a method Perform_exception associated with this class. We also define an object called Handler to store exceptions and to check them at the end of the transaction. The method Perform_exception analyzes the type of the exception

(IMMEDIATE or DEFERRED) and calls the Perform method associated to the exception (see later) or stores the exception in the object Handler. A method Final_perform is also generated to execute the method Perform on every exception in Handler at the end of the transaction.

2. Each time a new type of exception is defined (Define exception command), we generate a class with the name of the exception. This class is a subclass of the class Exception and its structure is the list of its parameters (to store the context of each exception raised). There are three methods in this class:

   (a) the method Affect that affects the attributes of the class when an exception is raised;

   (b) the method Perform that is the translation of the exception definition (a list of conditional statements);

   (c) the method Immediate that returns TRUE if the exception is of the type IMMEDIATE or false, otherwise.

3. The next step is the definition of a method with name out_M, where M is the name of the method with the out_context. As for the method in_M, the body of this method is the translation of the condition definition. For each condition, we generate a conditional statement with the following action associated:

   (a) create an object of the class corresponding to the raised exception;

   (b) assign the attributes of the object (a call to method Affect);

   (c) a call to method Perform_exception.

4. The last step is the generation of a call to the Final_perform method at the end of the transaction.

After these different steps, the schema is compiled by O2. At the moment, a simplified version of the generator runs on a Sun station. We have used Unix tools like Lex and Yacc to describe our grammar and to generate CO2 code. The main problem we have met is due to the fact that we used the O2 prototype and not the commercial product (a new version is currently under way using the O2 DBMS product). So, we did not have basic database features like commit and abort for transaction managing. This led us to write an interactive mechanism that displays errors and explains from which method the error is coming. This version of our prototype also uses a simplified language for condition, but shows the feasibility of our approach.

5 Conclusion

This paper addressed the problem of object oriented Databases consistency. According to the object paradigm, we advocated for expressing consistency as behavioral properties of objects, instead of considering database states. We proposed to express consistency control as pre and post-conditions to method execution. We distinguished between local control (i.e. at the level of the execution of one method) and global control (i.e. at the level of the execution of a transaction). Our language is inspired by SQL expressions and provides several flexible ways to control different kinds of consistency.

We made a complete experiment of our approach by implementing our propositions on top of the object oriented DBMS O2. We adopted a generation approach where the pre and post-conditions are translated into CO2 code which can run under the control of O2. We consider that this constitutes an original approach, but it is only one step towards better consistency control in future DBMS.

Our work can be extended in several directions. First, we have to incorporate our approach in the more general framework of an environment called Aristote, which is dedicated to persistent applications design and development [1]. In such an environment, the application developer is provided with a model and a DBPL which are available through highly interactive (graphic) interfaces.

The Aristote model provides specific constructs in order to make a clear distinction between intensional aspects (e.g. types) of an application and extensional aspects (e.g. persistent data, collections, class extensions). Using this model, the Aristote language can be used to express the source of the different application components. These source components are then translated by a generator in order to produce code able to run under a specific DBMS. We have already a generator and an application builder for O2. The Aristote language will be extended by adding the consistency aspects described in this paper.

Second, we think that dealing with consistency aspects needs a better formalization of object behavior and transaction concepts, in object oriented databases. Here, we want to study more formal aspects of rule's expression power and rule processing. Finally, we want to study the relationships between our approach and the area of active databases [21].

References

1. M. Adiba, C.Collet, P.Dechamboux, B.Defude,: Integrated tools for Object Oriented Persistent Application Development. DEXA Conf. Valence, September 1992

2. M. Atkinson, F. Bancilhon, D. De Witt, K. Dittrich, D. Maier, S. Zdonick: The Object Oriented Database System Manifesto. DOOD Conf. Kyoto, December 1989

3. N.S.Barghouti, G.E.Kaiser: Concurrency control in advanced database applications. ACM Computing Surveys, Vol. 23, No. 3, September 1991

4. A.P. Buchmann, R.S. Carrera, M.A. Vasquez-Galindo: A Generalized Constraint and Exception Handler for an Object oriented CAD-DBMS. Proc. of the Int. Workshop on Object oriented Database Systems, Pacific-Grove CA 23-26 September 1986

5. CACM: Special Issue: Next Generation DBMS. Com. of the ACM, Vol. 34, No. 10, October 1991

6. D. Cohen: Compiling complex database transition triggers. Proc. of the ACM SIGMOD Conf., Portland, Oregon, May 1989

7. U. Dayal, B. Blaustein, A. Buchmann, U. Chakravarthy, M. Hsu, R. Ledin, D. McCarthy, A. Rosenthal, S. Sarin: The HiPAC Project: Combining Active Databases and Timing Constraints. SIGMOD Record, Vol. 17, No. 1, March 1988

8. U. Dayal, M. Hsu, R. Ledin: A transaction model for long running activities. VLDB Int. Conf. 1991

9. B. Defude, H. Martin: Object oriented approach and new database application requirements. Proc. 4th. Int. Symp. on computer and information science ISCIS. Cesme Turkey, November 1989

10. O. Deux & al.: The story of O2. IEEE Trans. Knowl. Data Eng., Vol. 2, No. 1, March 1990

11. E. Dewayne, E. Perry: The Inscape program: Construction and evolution environment. Technical Report. AT&T Bell Laboratories, August 1986

12. K. Dittrich & al.: An Event/Trigger Mechanism to Enforce Complex Consistency Constraints in Design Databases. SIGMOD Record, Vol. 15, No. 3, September 1986

13. C. Esculier: Non monotonic knowledge evolution in VLKDBS. Proc. VLDB Conf., Brisbane, August 1990

14. A. Goldberg, D. Robson: Smalltalk-80: The Language and its Implementation. Addison- Wesley, Reading, MA 1983

15. C.A.R. Hoare: An Axiomatic Approach to computer programming. CACM pp 576-580 october 1969

16. C. Lecluse, P. Richard, F. Velez: O2, an object-oriented data model. Proc. of the SIGMOD Conf., Chicago, 1988

17. H. Martin: Controle de la cohérence dans les bases objets : une approche par le comportement. PhD Thesis Grenoble University, January 1991

18. B. Meyer: Object-oriented Software Construction. C.A.R. Hoare Series Editer 1988

19. J.M. Nicolas: Logic for improving Integrity Checking in Relational Data Bases. Acta Informatica Vol 18, Fasc. 3 December 1982

20. M. Stonebraker: Implementation of Integrity Constraints and Views by Query Modification. Int. Conf. on the management of data, Proc. of ACM- SIGMOD, San Jose CA May 1975

21. M.H. van der Voort, M.L. Kersten: Facets of Database Triggers. Report CS-R9122. CWI P.O. Box 4079, 1009 AB Amsterdam Netherlands, 1991

Integrity Constraints Representation in Object-Oriented Databases

A. Formica, M. Missikoff

IASI CNR - Viale Manzoni 30, I-00185 Rome, Italy

Abstract. This paper presents a Data Definition Language (DDL), called $\mathcal{TQL}$, based on an Object-Oriented data model characterized by the possibility of expressing integrity constraints in the schema of the database. This work originates from the need to enrich the amount of knowledge represented, declaratively, in the database schema and processed by the Database Management Systems (DBMS). The proposed approach allows the reduction of the amount of code in methods. However, by increasing the power of the DDL, the possibility of introducing errors in the schema also increases. Therefore, rich data models require enhanced checking facilities in order to support the design phase. In the paper, after having formally presented the language $\mathcal{TQL}$, the notions of satisfiability and correctness of a $\mathcal{TQL}$ schema, which are strictly related to the notion of legal database state, are introduced. These issues are presented using a formal approach based on a denotational semantics which concerns both the structural part of the schema and the integrity constraints.
Keywords: Integrity constraints, Object-Oriented database, database semantics, Typing, ISA Hierarchy.

1 Introduction

Database technology is steadily evolving towards richer database models and more powerful database systems (DBMS). This evolution aims at reducing the development cost of the application software. In the design phase, rich data models are sought to capture and describe a large part of the application domain in a declarative way. In the implementation phase, powerful DBMS primitives allow the further reduction of the burden of the code to be written.

Object-Oriented Databases (OODBs) represent a significant evolution with respect to traditional databases. Their evolution is both on the structural and on the behavioural levels. On the structural level, they embody the main features present in the proposals addressing the evolution of the relational model towards richer structures (NFNF [27], [6]), and the conceptual expressiveness of semantic data models [14]. On the behavioural level, OODB models have reached full Turing expressiveness with the introduction of methods. This last point allows the development of a full database application within a single paradigm avoiding, among others, the problem of

This research has been partially supported by "Progetto Finalizzato Sistemi Informatici e Calcolo Parallelo" of CNR, Subproject 5, Group Logidata+, and Subproject 6, Group Infokit.

impedance mismatch [3]. However, the increase of expressive power has in parallel introduced problems well known in the programming field, such as the cost of writing programs and problems related to their testability, reliability, maintainability.

It is widely recognized that in database applications a large portion of coding is represented by checks and verifications on the legality of the operations rather than their actual execution. If we can move a large number of integrity checks and enforcement functions into the DBMS, we will substantially reduce the amount of code required to implement a data-intensive application.

In this paper, we focus on the possibility of further enriching Object-Oriented data models by adding declarative integrity constraints to the schema of the database, liberating the application programmer from the necessity of coding them in the methods.

The goal of our work is to develop an Integrity Constraint Manager (ICM), conceived to process constraints at two levels. At a static level, during the design of the database, checks are performed in order to verify the correctness of the schema with constraints. At a dynamic level, during run-time processing, checks are performed in order to verify legal states of the database and to enforce data integrity in update operations.

This paper represents a first step toward a full-fledged, static and dynamic integrity constraint manager. In particular, we concentrate on the static part, i.e. the operations that ICM performs in the data definition phase. To this end we present $\mathcal{TQL}$, a language for OODB design which allows the specification of implicit and explicit integrity constraints in the schema of the database within a uniform, integrated data model.

In the next section, we review the main features of Object-Oriented data models and then briefly survey some results, from the literature, about integrity constraints. In Section 3, the constraint representation features of $\mathcal{TQL}$ are introduced, describing implicit, explicit, and inherent integrity constraints. About the latter, particular attention is posed on refinement constraints (ISA). In Section 4, the syntax of $\mathcal{TQL}$ and the notion of *schema* are formally presented. Finally, Section 5 introduces the formal semantics of the proposed language and the notions of *model* and *correctness* of a $\mathcal{TQL}$ schema.

2 Object-Oriented Data Model and Semantic Integrity Constraints

We assume the reader's familiarity with Object-Oriented databases. However, we review here those basic concepts that will be used subsequently in this paper, pointing out the specific features that characterize our proposal.

2.1 Main features of an Object-Oriented data model

<u>Objects</u> and <u>Values</u> - Objects are data structures composed of a state and an identifier (object identifier or *oid* for short). A state is represented by a structured set of labelled

oids organized in a tuple. The data model of $\mathcal{TQL}$ is based on the notion of *abstract object* as introduced in [5]. Abstract objects represent any conceivable conceptualization of real (and sometimes unreal) world entities, from a simple integer or string, such as 27 or "ferrari", to complex entities, such as persons and cars. There is a special class of "built-in" oids, such as integers or strings, on which the system is able to perform well defined manipulations. The oids of these "fully axiomatized" objects will be referred to as *values*. In this perspective, values are reduced to a special case of oids, i.e. identifiers of fully axiomatized elementary objects.

Object identity - This is a central notion for OODB models. Every object has an identity, given to it when created, unique within the database, and immutable throughout its lifetime. Oids allow the definition of complex objects in terms of other objects. Object sharing is a desirable characteristic that originates from the use of complex objects identifiers within tuples.

Complex objects - A complex object is defined by its relationships to other objects. These relationships are called properties and are organized in tuples. Tuples can be arbitrarily complex and are formed recursively using two constructors: tuple and set. Constructors can be nested to any (finite) depth (since we restrict the components to be only oids, we obtain complex objects inherently different from complex values [1], [17]). Conversely, elementary objects are values: they have the state that coincides with the oid. Therefore, values cannot be updated, they can be created and deleted.
For example, elementary objects (values) are:

34, ted, fiat, john, 21, math, 150.

Complex objects, representing a person, a car, and a student have oids:

#per12 , #car3, #stud1,

and a corresponding state, given respectively by:

[name:ted, age:34, vehicle:#car3],
[maker:fiat, speed:150] ,
[name:john, age:21, vehicle:#car3, dept: math] .

Note that, for sake of clarity, oids of complex objects are preceded by the symbol '#' (pound).

Cyclic objects - This is a characteristic common to expressive Object-Oriented data models, which allow the use of the oids of complex objects in a tuple. This mechanism allows a tuple to refer to another tuple which, in turn, can have a reference to the former. There are no limitations in the use of this mechanism, having also oids referencing their own structures (i.e. self-cyclic objects) or participating in a circular chain of arbitrary length.
For example consider the following objects:

(#emp12)   [name:john, salary:50K$, head_of: #d3]
(#d3)   [name:toys, floor: 4, manager: #emp12].

<u>Encapsulation</u> - This characteristic refers to the procedures attached to objects (methods) and to their internal state. It allows modularization of coding and enhanced protection of data. The behavioural component of the model is not explicitly addressed in this paper which, conversely, aims at the reduction of coding in the methods through a richer structural definition of the database, and the introduction of integrity constraints in the schema.

<u>Class</u> - Objects sharing common properties are gathered into a class. Classes are the repositories for objects. Therefore, they represent an extensional notion. Their counterpart at intensional level are types. In TQL data model, there is a tight correspondence between types and classes: there cannot exist two classes with the same type. This is a key feature of our proposal and its effects will be clarified later. Types are declared in the schema and represent a set of conditions (necessary and sufficient) for an object to be in the corresponding class. The dynamic part of a class includes mechanisms to create and destroy objects.

<u>Type</u> - A type is an abstract representation of the characteristics common to a set of objects. Given an object, it is always possible to decide whether it satisfies a type or not. A *type-definition* is a TQL expression having a label, a definition in the form of tuple of typed properties and, eventually, one or more integrity constraints associated to it. A *database schema* is represented by a collection of type-definitions, which includes integrity constraints. The objects entered in the database must be structured according to the types in the schema (unlike other systems, such as ORION [4], untyped objects are not allowed in TQL databases) and must satisfy the integrity constraints. The presence of type labels plays a primary role; they eliminate the use of class names in type-definitions (unlike, for example, O_2 [18], [19], [20]) thus allowing a clear separation between intensional and extensional components of the database.

For example, a schema for the objects defined in the preceding example is the following:

    mgr := [name:string, salary:string, head_of: dept]
    dept := [name:string, floor:integer, manager: mgr]

<u>Typed Properties</u> - In a type-definition, a property can be typed using: (i) a label of a user-defined type, (ii) an explicit set of values in parenthesis, (iii) a built-in type or (iv) a tuple of typed properties. Type labels allow object sharability at the extensional level while the last case allows the definition of nested tuple types whose instances will be nested object tuples not sharable by other objects. Properties can be multi-valued (indicated by curly brackets) and TQL allows explicit control over minimal and maximal cardinality of denoted sets. For example:

    student := [name:{string}$_{1,2}$, address:[street:string, city:string], dept:(math,cs,ee)].

<u>Recursive Types</u> - TQL allows a rich mechanism for recursion which mirrors the structure described for recursive objects. We have a self-recursive type when at least a property is typed using the same label of the type-definition. In general, recursion is

achieved when a type has a property typed with the label of a type-definition that, in turn, has a property typed with the former.

The following is an example of a self-recursive type:

person := [name:{string}$_{1,2}$, age:integer, child:{person}]

(note that cardinality constraints can be omitted).

Subtyping - Types are organized according to a generalization hierarchy, using the very powerful relation of subsumption [7], [11]. In TQL, the semantics of subsumption includes the three kinds of structured inheritance - inclusion, constraint, and specialization inheritance - introduced in existing OODB systems [3]. In TQL, subtyping can be explicitly declared by the user with the **ISA** construct, allowing the inheritance of properties and methods.

As an example, consider the following type-definition:

gr_student := **ISA** student [tutor:professor] .

2.2 Modeling constraints in database applications

Until now, we presented the most common features that can be found in current Object-Oriented data models. In the remainder of this paper, we introduce one of the main feature of TQL: the modeling of integrity constraints.

In contrast with the great demand of semantic integrity in database applications, there are few OODB systems [15] that provide the ability of declaring integrity constraints in the database schema using an extended data definition language and offering constraint management capabilities. This issue has been mainly addressed in relational and deductive databases areas. Let us briefly survey the literature in these areas.

In relational models, this problem has been widely studied. For example, in [8] integrity constraints have been formalized to provide a general purpose Constraint Specification Language which is a natural extension of the data definition language. In [24], a uniform model of integrity management is presented. It considers both validity and completeness of a relational database and also deals with the integrity of the answers produced by the queries. In [26], a knowledge-based approach has been proposed for efficient integrity enforcement. Other proposals rely on SQL and use the query language to express constraints and query processing techniques to verify integrity violation [9].

Deductive databases have been developed merging the two research areas of relational databases and logic programming. The aim of this database paradigm is to use a language based on Horn logic to query and reason about database content. In this area, integrity constraints are closed first order formulas that must be satisfied by the database [16], [2], [23].

As said before, the problem of expressing declarative constraints in an Object-Oriented data model has been tackled only by few authors, mainly interested in constraint enforcement. In particular, the language ALICE [30], [29] proposes a very powerful formalism for explicit constraints definition and a method for constraint analysis and run-time integrity enforcement. Another proposal is related to the PIROL project [12], developed to support engineering applications. Similarly, the ODE [13] system allows the definition of constraints and actions to be taken in presence of a violation. These proposals are very rich. However, their complexity precludes the possibility of investigating theoretical aspects and, in particular, to define a clear declarative semantics needed to develop tools to support database design.

With respect to the above proposals, this paper focuses mainly on the design phase of the database and proposes a Data Definition Language (DDL) enriched with integrity constraints. Through the study of the formal semantics of the language, we identify the properties that a well designed schema should have. As a further result of this study, we conceived a system able to automatically verify the correctness of a $\mathcal{TQL}$ schema: the ICM system. It is part of Mosaico [22], a design environment for Object-Oriented Knowledge Bases. A first prototype of Mosaico has been developed at IASI on Sun Workstation, using BIM-Prolog, and is currently being experimented.

3 Enriching OODB Schemas with Constraints

Traditionally, constraints are organized according to three sorts, namely: inherent, implicit, and explicit constraints [21], [28]. In Object-Oriented data models, inherent constraints, i.e. constraints that are imposed by the model itself, play an important role. They are refinement constraints related to the **ISA** constructor, or aggregation constraints related to typed properties. Furthermore, as a part of inherent constraints, we also deal with typing constraints, which impose type restrictions on the use of functions and comparison operators within explicit constraints (see below).

The language $\mathcal{TQL}$ allows the definition of implicit and explicit constraints. Implicit constraints, such as cardinality constraints or domain constraints, are expressed within the tuples in type-definitions. Explicit constraints are essentially comparison predicates defined over properties.

Let us first illustrate implicit and explicit integrity constraints modeling in $\mathcal{TQL}$. Refinement constraints will be discussed at the end of the section.

3.1 Implicit Constraints

Being expressed within tuples, implicit constraints are introduced through the typing mechanism of properties. Implicit constraints can be classified according to the following three cases.

- Cardinality constraints
On a multi-valued property, represented with curly brackets, it is possible to express constraints on the cardinality of the denoted set (minimal and maximal).
In the following example:

person := [name:{string}$_{1,3}$, age:integer, vehicle:{car}+].

the cardinality constraints on the property *name* impose that persons must have at least one and at most three names. If m,M represent the minimal and maximal cardinality respectively, the absence of curly brackets is a short-hand for m = 1 and M = 1, while curly brackets followed by the + symbol is a short form for and m = 1, M = ∞, and the absence of indexes means no cardinality constraints.

- Domain constraints

Domain constraints are imposed to properties that are typed using enumeration, in the form of a list, or an interval (in case of well ordered domains) defined using constant symbols.

In the following type-definition:

  car := [maker:(Fiat,Ford,BMW), m_speed:(120..200), owner:person].

the instances of the type *car* will be only cars produced by one of the three listed firms. Furthermore, the maximal speed will be any integer falling in the specified interval.

- Referential constraints

In the preceding section, we have seen that properties can be also typed using type labels. The type-definition in the above example indicates that a *car* object must be associated to an object of type *person*, through the property *owner*.

The absence of curly brackets imposes that each car must have one (and only one) owner which is a person.

3.2 Explicit Constraints

Explicit constraints are used to impose "θ-relationships" between two values or, more generally, two sets of objects (θ represents a comparison operator, such as "=", "<", ">",...) that are the terms of comparison. They are specified in the schema, being an integral part of type-definitions. Integrity constraints are expressed using the dot-notation formalism, which allows the construction of *paths*, i.e. chains of properties, one for each term of comparison. A "θ-constraint" is assumed to be universally quantified on the extension of the compared terms.

Consider the following set of type-definitions:

  person := [name:string, ssn:integer, phone:integer, age:integer,
                vehicle:car, child:{person}$_{1,5}$],
      ic1: this.ssn ≠ this.phone,
      ic2: this.ssn ≠ person.ssn,
      ic3: this.child.age < 10,
      ic4: this.vehicle.color = 'red'
  car := [maker:string, color:(red,green,blue)]
  teacher := **ISA** person [student:{person}+],
      ic5: this.student ≠ this.child
  employee := **ISA** person [salary:integer, boss:employee],
      ic6: this.salary ≤ this.boss.salary / 2 .

In this example, six explicit constraints are specified. An object that belongs to a given class, say *person*, must satisfy the constraints expressed in the corresponding type. In the comparison expression, the key-word "this" denotes the current object and a type label denotes the entire class (less the current object if we are comparing objects of the same class). In the above example, ic1 is a constraint imposed on the values of the current object in the class *person* (intra-object constraint), while ic2 compares the social security number of the current object with the same property of all the other objects in the same class (intra-class constraint). The constraint ic3 makes use of the dot-notation to navigate across objects. In particular, it imposes that the age of all the children of the current object must be less than a given constant (intra-class constraint). The constraint ic5 expresses that, for a *teacher*, his/her students and children must be different. This constraint involves a comparison between objects in the class *person*. Note that, since the θ operator is applied exhaustively to all the elements of the set denoted by a path, ic5 represents the disjunction of the two sets. Please note that the syntax requires a conjunctive form for the constraints, without loss of generality (any boolean condition can be represented in this form, after simple manipulations).

Dot-notation also allows a constraint to refer to other classes, and ic4 is an example of this possibility (inter-class constraint): it compares properties of objects in the class *car* referred by oids of the class *person*. When an arithmetic operator is used, it is applied to all the elements of the set denoted by a path. For this reason, the use of arithmetic operators is generally restricted to single-valued properties, as specified in ic6.

3.3 The ISA Hierarchy

In $\mathcal{TQL}$, the **ISA** construct is used to express (multiple) inheritance between types, indicating the supertypes from which a type inherits part of its definition (note that here we focus on the structural definition). Such a construct allows the definition of a refinement (subsumption) hierarchy of types. A refinement relationship among types correspond to set-containment among their corresponding extensions (i.e. classes). A type-definition which is not defined by means of the **ISA** construct is said to be in *normal form*. In particular, a type-definition which is not in normal form is *normal form reducible* (NF-reducible) if it can be transformed, applying inheritance, into an equivalent definition without **ISA**.

A type defined by means of the **ISA** construct inherits the typed properties of its supertypes. For each typed property, inheritance can be absolute, composed or refined. Inheritance is absolute if the property belongs to only one supertype and is not redefined in the subtype. Inheritance is composed if the property belongs to at least two supertypes. Finally, inheritance is refined if the property belongs to supertypes and to the definition of the subtype. If inheritance is absolute, the typed property is inherited without any modification. In the second case, a composition of typing for properties having the same name is required. Such a composition is obtained by considering a type (if there exists) that is a refinement of the given ones. Finally, in case of refined inheritance, an overriding is required. In particular, the typed properties of the supertypes will be overridden by the ones specified locally in the subtype, if the latter are refinement of the former.

In case of properties belonging to more than one supertype and locally redefined, composition is applied before overriding.

The above conditions determine the legality of the **ISA** hierarchy. For example, the following **ISA** hierarchy is legal:

person := [name:string, age:integer]
parent := **ISA** person [age:(10..150), child:{person}$_{1,5}$] .

In fact, in applying refined inheritance to the property *age*, the condition of refinement between the type *integer* and the set of values specified in the tuple is satisfied.

Refinement is violated in the following type-definitions:

vehicle := [maker:string, color:{(red,blue,green)}$_{1,3}$]
car := **ISA** vehicle [max_speed:integer, color:{(yellow,red)}$_{1,2}$] ,

because the types of the property *color* are not in refinement relationship.

Schemas having all type-definitions that are NF-reducible exhibit desirable properties. For example, the containment hierarchy of classes is automatically guaranteed and the placement of objects into classes is a deterministic operation.

4 The Database Definition Language $\mathcal{TQL}$

In this section, the syntax of the language $\mathcal{TQL}$ is formally presented, and the notion of database schema is given.

The language $\mathcal{TQL}$ is a direct derivation of $\mathcal{OOL}$, developed to analyze the relationships between Object-Oriented systems and Frame-based systems studied in Artificial Intelligence [25], [11]. A first proposal of $\mathcal{TQL}$ has been presented in [10].

4.1 $\mathcal{TQL}$ Syntax

In $\mathcal{TQL}$, we have terms and sentences. Terms can be *t_terms*, *p_terms*, and *c_terms*. A t_term is a type label. A p_term is a property name. A c_term is a constant, or a sequence of p_terms (*path*) preceded by a t_term or the keyword "this". Sentences can be *atomic*, *type-sentences*, *constraint expressions* and *type-definitions*. An atomic sentence is simply a name, e.g. car, person, color, integer, or an enumerated set, e.g. (4,8,9,22) or (red,green,yellow). A type-sentence is defined using two basic constructors (not mutually exclusive): **ISA** and tuple. A constraint expression is a boolean expression of binary integrity constraints. These are comparison predicates, taking two c_terms as arguments. A type-definition associates a t_term to a type-sentence or to an atomic sentence and, eventually, to one or more constraint expressions.

In the following boxes, the formal syntax of $\mathcal{TQL}$ is presented: non-terminal symbols are in small plain characters, while terminal symbol are in bold. Symbols in italics are user-defined strings.

Definition 4.1 Syntax of $\mathcal{TQL}$.

\<type-definition\> ::= t_term := \<s_type\> [, \<c_expr\>, ... , \<c_expr\>]

\<s_type\> ::= \<body\> | **ISA** t_term ... t_term \<body\>

\<body\> ::= t_term | \<bt\> | (\<$value\_set$\>) | [\<tp\>,...,\<tp\>]

\<bt\> ::= **integer** | **real** | **boolean** | **string** | **TOP**

\<tp\> ::= p_term:{\<body\>}$_{m,M}$ $\qquad\qquad$ m,M $\in \aleph_0 \cup \{\infty\}$ m ≤ M

In the above definition, s_type indicates the structural part of the type-definition. Among the built-in types (bt) there is the t_term **TOP** which stands for any possible type. The $value\_set$ construct can be expressed either by explicit enumeration or, in case of an interval, specifying upper and lower bounds.

Constraint expressions are now formally introduced. As already mentioned, they are boolean expressions of binary integrity constraints. A binary integrity constraint is a "θ-constraint" having the operands expressed using the dot-notation formalism. Dot-notation is a means to define explicit connections in the database schema that, at extensional level, identify the objects and properties on which the constraint must hold. Furthermore, dot-notation allows a path to be constructed as a composition of p_terms. It is also possible to use arithmetic functions in the comparison terms (c_terms). Therefore, in the syntax below, f stands for any arithmetic function which involves the operators "+", "-", "$*$", "/".

Definition 4.1 continued: constraint expressions.

\<c_expr\> ::= $label$: \<ic\>

\<ic\> ::= \<bin_ic\> | \<bin_ic\> **and** \<ic\> | \<bin_ic\> **or** \<ic\> | **not** \<ic\>

\<bin_ic\> ::= \<c_term1\> \<θ\> \<c_term2\>

\<c_term1\> ::= f (**this**.\<path\>)

\<c_term2\> ::= f (**this**.\<path\>) | f (t_term.\<path\>) | k

\<path\> ::= p_term. ... .p_term

\<θ\> ::= ≤ | ≥ | < | > | = | ≠

4.2 $\mathcal{TQL}$ Schemas

A non-empty set of type-definitions is *fully defined* (*defined* for short) iff: i) there are no dangling t_terms, ii) paths in constraint expressions are compatible with the definition of the associated tuples. Therefore, we have the following definition:

Definition 4.2 *TQL schema*.
A *TQL schema* is a *defined* set of type-definitions. □

For example, consider the set of type-definitions:

> person := [name:string, age:integer, child:{person}]
>   ic1: this.age > this.child.weight
> adult := **ISA** person employee [name:string, age:(31..150)]
> student := **ISA** person [age:(17..40), college:university]

This is not a schema because the second path, in the constraint expression ic1, is not compatible with the tuple associated to the t_term *person*. Furthermore, in the second and third type-definitions respectively, *employee* and *university* are dangling t_terms: they are not type labels of any type-definition.

5 Formal Semantics of TQL

The semantics of TQL reported here follows a pure denotational approach. Within this approach a schema is a set of formulas (type-definitions) and a database state is simply one of its possible interpretations. Given an interpretation, types and classes have a functional correspondence: for each type there is only one class that corresponds to it. In our approach, a database update causes a transition from an interpretation to another one. The formalism presented below has been influenced by [7], and derives from preliminary work carried out in comparing OODB systems and terminological knowledge representation systems in Artificial Intelligence [25], [11].

Definition 5.1 The semantics of type-definitions.
Let Σ be a finite set of oids representing a given state of the Application Domain, T the set of TQL expressions, and P the set of p_terms. Consider a function $\mathcal{E}$ from T to the powerset $\wp(\Sigma)$:

$$\mathcal{E} : T \rightarrow \wp(\Sigma)$$

and a function Π from P to the powerset $\wp(\Sigma \times \Sigma)$:

$$\Pi : P \rightarrow \wp(\Sigma \times \Sigma).$$

Then, $\mathcal{E}$ is an *extension function* over Σ with respect to the type-definition:

$$t\_term_a := s\_type \, [, c\_expr, \ldots , c\_expr]$$

iff the values of $\mathcal{E}$ on s_type and constraint expressions are constructed starting from the values of their components as follows.
To make it clearer, we compute the extension of an s_type following the structure of the syntax:

$\mathcal{E}\{s\_type\} =$
   a) $\mathcal{E}\{body\}$
   b) $\mathcal{E}\{\textbf{ISA}\ t\_term_1 \ldots t\_term_n\ body\} = (\cap_i \mathcal{E}\{t\_term_i\}) \cap \mathcal{E}\{body\}$

$\mathcal{E}\{body\} =$
   c) $\mathcal{E}\{t\_term\}$

d) $\mathcal{E}\{bt\}$

e) $\mathcal{E}\{(value\_set)\} = \{value\_set\} \cap \Sigma$

f) $\mathcal{E}\{[tp_1,...,tp_r]\} = \cap_j \mathcal{E}\{[tp_j]\}$

$\mathcal{E}\{bt\} =$

g) $\mathcal{E}\{\textbf{integer}\} = \mathbb{Z} \cap \Sigma$

h) $\mathcal{E}\{\textbf{real}\} = \mathbb{R} \cap \Sigma$

i) $\mathcal{E}\{\textbf{boolean}\} = \{true, false\} \cap \Sigma$

l) $\mathcal{E}\{\textbf{string}\} = \mathbb{S} \cap \Sigma$

m) $\mathcal{E}\{\textbf{TOP}\} = \Sigma$

$\mathcal{E}\{[tp]\} = \mathcal{E}\{[p\_term:\{body\}_{m,M}]\} = E_1 \cap E_2$

where:

$E_1 = \{ x \in \Sigma \mid \forall y \in \Sigma : <x,y> \in \Pi\{p\_term\} \Rightarrow y \in \mathcal{E}\{body\} \}$

$E_2 = \{ x \in \Sigma \mid m \leq |S_{p\_term,x}| \leq M \}$

with: $m, M \in \aleph_0 \cup \{\infty\}$,

$S_{p\_term,x} = \{ y \in \Sigma \mid <x,y> \in \Pi\{p\_term\} \}$,

and $|S_{p\_term,x}|$ represents the cardinality of the set $S_{p\_term,x}$.

It is easy to verify that if a type-sentence is NF-reducible, then its extension, as defined at the point (b), is equivalent to the extension of the tuple obtained after such a reduction, as defined at the point (f) of the above definition.

With respect to constraint expressions, we describe here the semantics of the basic binary forms. The three forms reported in the following concern respectively: comparison where the two paths originate from the same object, comparison where the right term ranges over a whole class, comparison against a constant.

$\mathcal{E}\{c\_expr\} = \mathcal{E}\{label : bin\_ic\} = \mathcal{E}\{label : c\_term1 \; \theta \; c\_term2\} =$

i) $\mathcal{E}\{label : f(\textbf{this}. \; p\_term_1. \; ... \; .p\_term_n) \; \theta \; g(\textbf{this}. \; q\_term_1. \; ... \; .q\_term_m)\} =$
$$= \{x \in \Sigma \mid \quad \forall (y_1,..., y_n) : \langle x,y_1\rangle \in \Pi\{p\_term_1\},$$
$$\langle y_1,y_2\rangle \in \Pi\{p\_term_2\}, ... , \langle y_{n-1},y_n\rangle \in \Pi\{p\_term_n\},$$
$$\forall (z_1,..., z_m) : \langle x,z_1\rangle \in \Pi\{q\_term_1\},$$
$$\langle z_1,z_2\rangle \in \Pi\{q\_term_2\}, ... , \langle z_{m-1},z_m\rangle \in \Pi\{q\_term_m\}$$
$$\Rightarrow f(y_n) \; \theta \; g(z_m)\}$$

ii) $\mathcal{E}\{label : f(\textbf{this}. \; p\_term_1. \; ... \; .p\_term_n) \; \theta \; g(t\_term_b. \; q\_term_1. \; ... \; .q\_term_m)\} =$
$$= \{x \in \Sigma \mid \quad \forall (y_1,..., y_n) : \langle x,y_1\rangle \in \Pi\{p\_term_1\},$$
$$\langle y_1,y_2\rangle \in \Pi\{p\_term_2\}, ... , \langle y_{n-1},y_n\rangle \in \Pi\{p\_term_n\},$$
$$\forall (z, z_1,..., z_m) : z \in \mathcal{E}\{t\_term_b\},$$
$$z \neq x \text{ if } t\_term_a = t\_term_b, \langle z,z_1\rangle \in \Pi\{q\_term_1\},$$
$$\langle z_1,z_2\rangle \in \Pi\{q\_term_2\}, ... , \langle z_{m-1},z_m\rangle \in \Pi\{q\_term_m\}$$
$$\Rightarrow f(y_n) \; \theta \; g(z_m)\}$$

iii) $\mathcal{E}\{label : f(\textbf{this}. \; p\_term_1. \; ... \; .p\_term_n) \; \theta \; k \} =$
$$= \{x \in \Sigma \mid \quad \forall (y_1,..., y_n) : \langle x,y_1\rangle \in \Pi\{p\_term_1\},$$
$$\langle y_1,y_2\rangle \in \Pi\{p\_term_2\}, ... , \langle y_{n-1},y_n\rangle \in \Pi\{p\_term_n\}$$
$$\Rightarrow f(y_n) \; \theta \; k \}$$

The symbols f and g represent any functions defined by means of arithmetic operators. In ii), t_term_b is any type label and t_term_a is the label of the type-definition we are analyzing. $\square$

Definition 5.2 *Interpretation* of a $\mathcal{TQL}$ schema.
An *interpretation* of a $\mathcal{TQL}$ schema is a 3-tuple $\Im = <\Sigma,\mathcal{E},\Pi>$ where Σ represents the Application Domain, Π is a function as defined above, and $\mathcal{E}$ is an extension function over Σ with respect to each type-definition of the schema. $\square$

Definition 5.3 *Model* of a $\mathcal{TQL}$ schema.
A *model* of a $\mathcal{TQL}$ schema is an interpretation $\Im = <\Sigma,\mathcal{E},\Pi>$ such that, for each type-definition in the schema:
$$t\_term := s\_type\ [,\ c\_expr_1,\ \dots\ ,\ c\_expr_k]$$
it results:
$$\mathcal{E}\{t\_term\} = \mathcal{E}\{s\_type\}\ [\cap\ (\cap_j\ \mathcal{E}\{c\_expr_j\})].$$
$\square$

Given the formal semantics of the $\mathcal{TQL}$ language, let us introduce some definitions related to the notion of *class* and *correctness* of a schema.

Definition 5.4 *Class* of a type-definition.
Given a model $\Im = <\Sigma,\mathcal{E},\Pi>$ for the type-definition:
$$t\_term := s\_type\ [,\ c\_expr_1,\ \dots\ ,\ c\_expr_k]$$
the set of oids represented by:
$$\mathcal{E}\{t\_term\}\ (=\mathcal{E}\{s\_type\}\ [\cap\ (\cap_j\ \mathcal{E}\{c\_expr_j\})])$$
is the *class* of the type-definition under such a model. $\square$

For example, consider the schema:

person := [name:{string}$_{1,2}$, age:(0..150), vehicle:car],
      ic: this.vehicle.color = 'red'
car := [maker:string, color:(red,green,yellow)]

and the following model, $\Im = <\Sigma,\mathcal{E},\Pi>$, of this schema:

$\Sigma = \{\#p1,\#p2,\#c1,\#c2,41,70,Tom,John,Mary, Fiat,Alfa,red,green\}$

$\mathcal{E}\{person\} = \{\#p1\}$
$\mathcal{E}\{car\} = \{\#c1,\#c2\}$

$\Pi\{age\} = \{<\#p1,41>, <\#p2,70>\}$
$\Pi\{color\} = \{<\#c1,red>, <\#c2,green>\}$
$\Pi\{maker\} = \{<\#c1,Fiat>, <\#c2,Alfa>\}$
$\Pi\{name\} = \{<\#p1,Tom>, <\#p1,John>, <\#p2,Mary>\}$
$\Pi\{vehicle\} = \{<\#p1,\#c1>, <\#p2,\#c2>\}.$

Since this is a model, for the first expression it results:

$\mathcal{E}\{person\} =$
$\mathcal{E}\{[name:\{string\}_{1,2}, age:(0..150), vehicle:car]\} \cap \mathcal{E}\{this.vehicle.color = 'red'\}.$

Therefore, the class of the first type-definition, under this model, is given by the set:

$\mathcal{E}\{\text{person}\} = \{\#p1\}$.

Similarly, the class of the second type-definition is the following:

$\mathcal{E}\{\text{car}\} = \{\#c1,\#c2\}$.

Now, we introduce the notions of *satisfiability* of a type-definition and *correctness* of a schema.

Definition 5.5 *Satisfiability* of a type-definition.
The type-definition:

$$t\_term := s\_type [, c\_expr_1, \dots , c\_expr_k]$$

is *satisfiable* iff:
i)   it does not violate typing constraints, whenever its definition contains explicit integrity constraints;
ii) there exists at least one model $\mathfrak{S} = <\Sigma,\mathcal{E},\Pi>$ under which the corresponding class is non-empty:

$$\mathcal{E}\{t\_term\} \neq \emptyset.$$

□

Definition 5.6 *Correctness* of a $\mathcal{TQL}$ schema.
A $\mathcal{TQL}$ schema is *correct* iff there exists at least one model $\mathfrak{S} = <\Sigma,\mathcal{E},\Pi>$ for the schema, under which all the type-definitions have non-empty class. □

Let us analyze an example of an incorrect schema. Consider the following set of type-definitions:

person := [name:{(Tom,Mary)}$_{3,4}$, child:person],
adult := [name:(Tom,Mary), owner_of:car],
        ic1: this.owner_of.color = 'yellow'
vehicle := [speed:integer, type:string],
        ic2: this.speed/2 > this.type
car := [speed:integer, color:(red,green,blue)]

This schema is not correct because of the unsatisfiability of the type-sentences associated to the t_terms *person, adult* and *vehicle*. In particular, the first two type-definitions violate point (ii) of the definition 5.5. In fact, the former has always empty extension because the minimal cardinality constraint defined on the property *name* is inconsistent with the cardinality of its enumerated type. Similarly for the latter, since the color required in the constraint ic1 does not belong to the set of colors allowed for the type *car*.
The type-definition *vehicle* violates inherent typing constraints (point (i) of definition 5.5), because of comparison between two terms having incompatible types.

6 Conclusion

In this paper, we presented the data definition language $\mathcal{TQL}$, with advanced features in representing both implicit and explicit integrity constraints. We believe that enriching an OODB system with integrity management capability will reduce the cost of developing database applications. Enriching the expressive power of the DDL requires, at the same time, a clear understanding of what correct database schemas are, in order to supply a tool to support the database designer. Having this goal in mind, we developed a formal semantics, based on a denotational approach, which allowed the formal definition of database schema, interpretation of a schema (corresponding to a database state), model of a schema (corresponding to a legal database state), and correctness of a schema. These definitions are the basis of the specifications for a module of the System Mosaico: the ICM devoted to the schema verification. A first prototype of this module has been implemented in BIM-Prolog on Sun workstation. It is able to process a set of type-definitions in order to determine if it represents a correct $\mathcal{TQL}$ schema, giving useful diagnostics if it fails. Currently, we are working in order to determine the complexity of the related algorithm.

$\mathcal{TQL}$ represents a compromise between expressive power and possibility of automatic validation of schema design. In the near future, we intend to investigate the possibility of extending the support given to the database designer. In particular, we are considering the evolution of the ICM system that, whenever a schema is detected incorrect, will be able to "repair" the faulty schema, either automatically (in simpler cases) or interactively, asking the help of the database designer.

References

1. S.Abiteboul, C.Beeri, "On the power of Languages for Manipulating Complex Objects", International Workshop on Theory and Applications of Nested Relations and Complex Objects, Darmstadt, 1987.

2. P. Asirelli, P. Inverardi, A. Mustaro, "Improving Integrity Constraint Checking in Deductive Databases", Lecture Notes in Computer Science 326, 72-86, ICDT'88, 1988.

3. M.Atkinson, F.Bancilhon, D.DeWitt, K.Dittrich, D.Maier, S.Zdonik, "The Object-Oriented Database System Manifesto", Technical Report, Altair 30-89, 1989.

4. J.Banerjee, H.Chou, J.F.Garza, W.Kim, D.Woelk, N.Ballou, "Data Model Issues for Object-Oriented Applications", Readings in Database Systems, M.Stonebraker (Ed.), Morgan Kaufmann Pub., 1988.

5. C.Beeri, "A formal approach to object-oriented databases", Data & Knowledge Engineering 5, 353-382, North-Holland, 1990.

6. F.Bancilhon, S.Khoshafian, "A calculus for complex objects", Proc. of ACM SIGACT-SIGMOD Symp. on Principles of Database Systems, 1986.

7. R.J.Brachman, H.J.Levesque, "The tractability of Subsumption in Frame-Based Description Languages", Proc. of National Conference on Artificial Intelligence - AAAI 84, 34-37, Austin, 1984.

8. E.Bertino, D.Musto, "Correctness of Semantic Integrity Checking in Database Management Systems", Acta Informatica 26, 25-57, 1988.

9. S.Ceri, J.Widom, "Deriving Production Rules for Constraint Maintenance", Proc. of the 16th VLDB Conference, Brisbane, Australia 1990.

10. A.Formica, M.Missikoff, "Materialization of recursive objects in Object-Oriented Databases", Proc. of the Ninth International Symposium Applied Informatics, Innsbruck, 1991.

11. A.Formica, M.Missikoff, S.Vazzana, "An Object-Oriented Data Model for Artificial Intelligence Applications", Next Generation Information Systems Technology, LNCS 504, Springer Verlag, 1991.

12. R.Gernert, N.Greif, "Modelling of Complex Objects and Semantic Integrity Constraints in Product Databases", Informatik Informationem - Report No.2/1990, Berlin 1990.

13. N.Gehani, H.V.Jagadish, "Ode as an Active Database: Constraints and Triggers", Proc. of the 17th VLDB Conference, Barcelona, Sept. 1991.

14. R.Hull, R.King, "Semantic data modeling: survey, applications and research issues", ACM Computing Survey 19.

15. J.G.Hughes, "Object-Oriented Databases", Prentice Hall, Cambridge, 1991.

16. R. Kowalski, F.Sadri, P.Soper, "Integrity Checking In Deductive Databases", Proc. of the 13th VLDB Conference, 61-69, Brighton, 1987.

17. G.M.Kuper, M.Y.Vardi, "A New Approach to Database Logic", Proc. of ACM Symposium on Principles on Database Systems, 1984.

18. C.Lecluse, P.Richard, "The O_2 database programming language", Proc. of VLDB '89 Conference, Amsterdam, 1989.

19. C.Lecluse, P.Richard, "Modeling Complex Structures in Object-Oriented Databases", Proc. of ACM PODS Conference, 1989.

20. C.Lecluse, P.Richard, F.Velez, "O_2: an Object-Oriented Data Model", Proc. of ACM SIGMOD Conference, Chicago, 1988.

21. D.C.Tsichritzis, F.H.Lochovsky, "Data Models", Prentice-Hall, Englewood Cliffs, 1982.

22. M.Missikoff, H.Lam, "Mosaico: A Specification and Rapid Prototyping Environment for Object-Oriented Database Applications", Technical Note December 1992.

23. G.Moerkotte, S.Karl, "Efficient Consistency Control in Deductive Databases", Lecture Notes in Computer Science 326, 118-128, ICDT'88, 1988.

24. A.Motro, "Integrity = Validity + Completeness", ACM Transactions on Database Systems, Vol.14, No.4, 480-502, December 1989.

25. M.Missikoff, S.Vazzana, "*OOL*: an Object Oriented Language for Knowledge Representation", Proc. of IV International Symposium on Knowledge Engineering, Barcelona, May 1990.

26. X.Qian, G.Wiederhold, "Knowledge-based Integrity Constraint Validation", Proc. of the 12th VLDB Conference, Kyoto, Japan 1986.

27. H.J.Schek, M.H.Scholl, "The Relational Model with Relation-Valued Attributes", Information Systems, Vol.11, No.2, 1986.

28. A.Shepherd, L.Kerschberg, "Constraint Management in Expert Database Systems", Proc. of First Int'l Workshop on Expert Database Systems, L. Kerschberg (Ed.), Benjamin/Cummings Publ., Menlo Park, 1986.

29. S.D. Urban, L.M.L. Delcambre, "Constraint Analysis: a Design Process for Specifying Operations", Transactions on Knowledge and Data Engineering, March 1991.

30. S.D. Urban, "ALICE: An Assertion Language for Integrity Constraint Expression", COMPSAC Proceedings, Orlando, September 1989.

A Framework for Temporal Object Databases

Niki Pissinou[1] and Kia Makki[2]

[1] National Supercomputing Center For Energy And The Environment,
University of Nevada, Las Vegas NV89154
[2] Department of Computer Science, University of Nevada, Las Vegas NV89154

Abstract. The 3 Dimensional Information Space (3DIS) is a rich, extensible, object database model for information management. Here, we concentrate on extending the 3DIS to incorporate the semantics of time, and to support temporal data and the temporal evolution of data. We present a unique approach towards the synthesis of an integrated 3DIS model that supports the temporal aspects of data modeling in addition to the structural and dynamic ones, while preserving its original three dimensional geometric space features. This research presents a step towards defining the concepts and techniques for incorporating time in object databases, and provides a concrete experimental framework for demonstration thereof.

1 Introduction

There are currently many data models that have powerful modeling constructs designed to make the tasks of database design, evolution, and manipulation simple and easy for database designers and users [1, 3]. But most of these models do not provide adequate support for representing temporal information. Traditional database management systems that embody these models are therefore limited in their ability to directly record and process time-varying aspects of the "real world." Such databases represent only "current facts." They do not incorporate the concept of time or provide support for the representation of temporal information. For example, a database records only the most current value of an object's attributes, and when those values change their previous values are erased.

There has been growing awareness among researchers of the importance of recording historical information in a database [2]. With these approaches, more complete information of the dynamics of a database's application environment is retained. The vast majority of research on temporal database systems is on relational and pseudo-relational database models, and has focused on the extension of such models to incorporate time. Little attention has been given to the temporal aspects of objects for semantic and object database models[3].

Our goal here is the design and experimental validation of a higher level object database model that will enable the database designer to naturally and

---

[3] We use the term object "database" to refer to one which incorporates such characteristics as individual object identity, explicitly semantic primitives, active objects and object uniformity.

directly incorporate the semantics of time into a conceptual schema. Such a "temporal object database" description and formalism is intended to serve as a natural application modeling mechanism to capture and express the temporal aspects of the application environment in addition to the structural and behavioral ones. Our work represents a first step towards the synthesis of an integrated object data model that supports the temporal aspects of data.

Specifically, we extend the 3DIS (3 dimensional information space) [1] to support temporal data and the temporal evolution of data. Our approach consists of designing a temporal 3DIS model and developing an experimental prototype for validation of our work. We have chosen the 3DIS for two main reasons: First, the 3DIS model includes prominent and desired features from semantic and object-oriented database models. For example, objects at various levels of abstraction and granularity are accommodated, inter-object relationships are supported and a pre-defined set of abstractions is provided. Second, the geometric space representation of the 3DIS seems to be a natural environment for adding time. This space is a 3-dimensional geometric representation of information triplets (domain object, mapping-object, range-object); triplets are used to model all meta-data. Our work presents a unique approach towards the synthesis of an integrated 3DIS model that supports the temporal aspects of data modeling in addition to the structural and behavioral ones, while preserving its original three dimensional geometric space features.

The remainder of this paper is organized as follows: In the next section we present a brief a specification of the 3DIS. In section 3, we present the temporal 3DIS model, and show how temporal data and the evolution of temporal data is represented in this framework. In the last section we formulate some conclusions.

2 A Specification of the 3DIS

Our approach to temporal data in the object database context is based upon a generic object database model called the 3DIS. As described in [1], the 3DIS is an extensible, object-oriented framework for information management designed for data-intensive information system applications in which information objects of various levels of abstraction and modalities must be accommodated and descriptive and meta-data is rich and dynamic. As such, the 3DIS provides an approach in which data and the descriptive information about data are handled uniformly in an extensible framework.

The 3DIS supports two basic modeling constructs: *objects* (atomic, type and composite) and *mappings*. Mappings are a special kind of composite object and are used for modeling relations among two objects. Thus relationships among objects are modeled by (domain-object, mapping-object, range-object) triples [1]. In a 3DIS database all information (data, meta-data, abstractions, operations and constraints) is treated uniformly as objects. Basic associations among objects are enacted though a set of predefined abstraction primitives such as basic data/meta-data relationships. The basic data definition and data manipulation operations are supported by a small and simple set of specification operations.

The 3DIS geometric representation is used to represent and organize database objects and their interrelationships graphically [1].

Although the 3DIS is a rich, extensible object database model for information management, support for temporal data and the temporal evolution of data within the 3DIS framework continues to be a major requirement. In the following section we show how the 3DIS can be extended to incorporate the semantics of time and support the temporal evolution of data.

3 The Temporal 3DIS (T-3DIS) Model

Temporal 3DIS (T-3DIS) databases contain collections of inter-related temporal and non-temporal objects, where all information including the data, the descriptions, classifications and temporal behavior of data (meta-data), abstractions, operations, and constraints are treated uniformly as objects at various discrete time intervals. Within this "temporal object-based" framework, the T-3DIS incorporates several predefined fundamental temporal abstraction primitives in addition to the ones provided by the 3DIS. T-3DIS is further extended to support a number of other abstractions that are commonly needed in application environments where the representation of temporal data and evolution of temporal data plays a significant role. A set of temporal operations is defined on objects that allows uniform viewing, insertion, deletion, and modification of temporal objects in a T-3DIS database.

In what immediately follows we describe a set of principles to which the T-3DIS model must adhere and introduce some preliminary concepts and definitions. We also describe the T-3DIS in terms of its modeling constructs, its predefined and extended abstraction mechanisms, and its object manipulation primitives.

3.1 The Design of T-3DIS

The T-3DIS has been designed to meet a number of criteria which we believe to be essential in an effective temporal object database description and structuring formalism. They are as follows:

1. The T-3DIS (a temporal object model) should be a consistent extension of 3DIS (a non-temporal object model).
2. The T-3DIS should not only allow us to describe the time-invariant meaning and properties of an object, but also specify and relate different time-varying aspects of that object.
3. At any given time, either an event or its negation (but not both) can be "active" in the T-3DIS. This also applies to the duration of an event.
4. The T-3DIS should capture and describe events as they occur in the application environment it attempts to represent, and incorporate different views of the same information.
5. The T-3DIS should tolerate incomplete information for certain periods of time.

6. In addition to the information provided to the database at various points in time, there should be a set of operations that enable the inference of certain properties at other points of time not explicitly recorded.

7. The T-3DIS should support temporal derived data.

These principles provide a general view of the characteristics of our temporal 3DIS model. In the following sections we show how the 3DIS model can be extended to incorporate temporal data while still preserving these characteristics.

3.2   Temporal Object Semantic Concepts

We now present some concepts and definitions necessary for the specification of our approach to extending the 3DIS to incorporate the semantics of time. To describe the structure of an object as it evolves over time and across its multiple representations (i.e., versions and history) we introduce the notions of *universal object identity* and *possible object world*. Together these two notions allows us to describe the meaning, characteristics, properties, behavior and role of each individual object at different times and at a particular point in time.

Definition. The *Universal Object Identity* of an object, denoted as UOI, refers to an object's interpretation or sense and remains time invariant.

Definition. The *Possible Object World* of an object, denoted as POW, refers to an object's denotation and is usually time variant.

Example. The universal object identity of the temporal object "fight" would be a struggle but its possible object world could be an emotional struggle, physical struggle, quarrel, contest etc.

An object cannot have a possible object world unless its universal object identity is defined. An object can have different possible object worlds at different times, and also several possible object worlds at a particular time. For example, the object "fight" could be a physical struggle in 1989 followed by an emotional struggle in 1990. Also the object "fight" can concurrently be a physical and an emotional struggle. In general, a universal object identity encapsulates the time invariant semantic meaning of an object, while a possible object world encapsulates the static and dynamic structure, behavior and role of each individual object at different temporal intervals.

Further, the UOI of an object can be derived from all its possible POWs at all different times with respect to our model and the world we are modeling by taking the union of possible POWs over time. Thus, we can formally define the UOI of an object from all its possible POWs at all different times with respect to POWs, our database model and the world we are modeling, as follows:

$$UOI_\alpha \, (M) \; =_{def} \; \{ \, t \rightarrow POW_\alpha(M,t) \mid t \in T \, \}$$

where UOI is the universal object identity of an object, POW_α is the possible object world of an object α, M is our database model, and $t \in T$ is the time a possible object world is active (current).

The above definition assumes that users interact with only a single world during a time period. When users interact with different worlds then the UOI of an object is defined as follows:

$$UOI_\alpha(M) =_{def} \{< w,t > \rightarrow POW_\alpha(M,w,t)| \ w \in W \ \text{and} \ t \in T \}$$

where UOI_α, POW_α and M are as defined previously, and $w \in W$ is the "miniworld" we are modeling (may be assumed to be a version.)

The simple, generic set of definitions described in this section may be used as the basis for the specification and stepwise development of database models and database systems of increasing complexity. To demonstrate this, in the next section we concentrate on extending an existing object model, the 3 Dimensional Information Space (the 3DIS [1]), to incorporate the semantics of time, and to support temporal data and the temporal evolution of data. The T-3DIS (Temporal - 3 Dimensional Information Space) draws from notions introduced here and in [5, 6, 7]. We describe the T-3DIS in terms of its modeling constructs, its predefined and extended abstraction mechanisms, and its object manipulation primitives.

3.3 Modeling Constructs

The T-3DIS model extends the 3DIS model to include temporal information on objects, mappings and types. Each object is associated with a *temporal version*, $\{[t_a, t_b], \{versionnumbers\}\}$ which gives the *lifespan* of an object for a given version or a sequence of versions (the later case occurring when an object's existence persists over several versions.) The default version is represented as v_0. By augmenting the version number with a time interval we capture the evolution of an object.

We adopt the notion of a *time interval* [4], $[t_a, t_b]$ where t_a is a first time instant and t_b is the last time instant of the time interval. When the last time instant of the time interval is the current time, this is denoted as $[t_a, \infty]$. A single discrete time point t is denoted as $[t_a, t_a]$. The time interval of non-temporal objects is denoted as $([0, 0], 0)$. To more accurately represent temporal data and the evolution of temporal objects, it is desirable to model different time dimensions such as valid, transaction and user-defined times. For simplicity in representing this information and in developing an initial experimental prototype we consider only valid time, but the other two kinds of time can easily be incorporated into the model. A possible way for accomplishing this is to slightly extend our definition of a temporal version to incorporate these kinds of time. In such a case we will define a *total temporal version* as follows {*valid time temporal version, transaction time temporal version, user-defined temporal version* }. A valid time temporal version is a temporal version whose time interval denotes the valid time. Similar definitions apply to the transaction and user-defined temporal versions.

Relationships among objects are modeled by

"(domain-object($[t_i, t_j], v$), mapping-object($[t_k, t_l], v$), range-object($[t_m, t_n], v$))"

triples where: t_i, t_k and t_m are each a "first time instant," and t_j, t_l and t_n are each a "last time instant," for the domain-object, mapping object and range object respectively. Here v indicates a version number.

In the T-3DIS we represent the temporal behavior of relationships and deduce temporal inter-object relationships through the mappings by attaching to the mapping-object a "time interval." Thus a single-valued temporal binary relationship stating "the telephone number of James is 743 from 1980-1990", is represented by a *temporal simple triple:* [4] (James([50,∞],1), HasNo ([80,90],1), 743([80,90],1). The temporal version of the mapping object ([80,90],1) represents the temporal relationship between James and his telephone number. In this way we can determine the *lifespan of a mapping* which in turn allows us to determine temporal inter-object relationships. A multi-valued temporal binary relationship stating "the phone numbers of Emp_1 are 743 and 740" may be represented by the two simple triples:

$$(\mathbf{Emp_1}([50, \infty], 1), \mathbf{HasNo}([80, 90], 1), 743([80, 90], 1)),$$
$$(\mathbf{Emp_1}([50, \infty], 1), \mathbf{HasNo}([85, 90], 1), 743([85, 90], 1)),$$

or by the single *temporal compound triple:*

$$(\mathbf{Emp_1}([50, \infty], 1), \mathbf{HasNo}([80, 90], 1), \{743([80, 90], 1), 740([85, 90], 1)\}).$$

A temporal compound triple contains a set as one of its three elements. Triples with more than one set element are not allowed, since in general the semantics of the relationships among the elements of the two sets is ambiguous. There are certain temporal constraints associated with temporal compound triples. For example, the first and last time instances of the temporal version of the mapping object should be within a range of the first and last time instances of the temporal version of the domain and range objects.

As in the case of the 3DIS, in the T-3DIS temporal n-ary relationships among objects (where n > 2) are handled by defining a new object to represent the n-ary relationship itself, and then a set of temporal binary relationships between that new object and all objects involved in the original n-ary relationship. For example, a contract is a relationship that can involve more than two objects, e.g., a buyer $\mathbf{A}([1920,1991],1)$, a seller $\mathbf{B}([1960,1991],1)$, a property $\mathbf{C}([1969,\infty],1)$, and a price $\$18$ ([0,0],1). These facts are modeled by introducing a new object $\mathbf{Con}$. Then, the buyer(A), the seller(B), the property(C), and the price are related to this contract as follows:

$$(\mathbf{Con}([1980, 1980], 1), \mathbf{Buy}([1980, 1980], 1), \mathbf{A}([1920, 1991], 1)),$$
$$(\mathbf{Con}([1980, 1980], 1), \mathbf{Sell}([1980, 1980], 1), \mathbf{B}([1960, 1991], 1)),$$
$$(\mathbf{Con}([1980, 1980], 1), \mathbf{Property}([1980, 1980], 1), \mathbf{C}([1969, \infty], 1)),$$
$$(\mathbf{Con}([1980, 1980], 1), \mathbf{Price}([1980, 1980], 1), \$18([0, 0], 1))$$

The decomposition of temporal n-ary relations into their irreducible binary relations has not proven to be a limitation in capturing the semantics of temporal n-ary relations.

---

[4] In these examples only the last two digits of a year are shown, e.g.,50 instead of 1950.

Temporal Objects As in the 3DIS, every identifiable information fact in an application environment corresponds to a *temporal object* in a T-3DIS database. Consequently, the generic notion of temporal objects represents all modeling concepts described above. Simple, compound, and behavioral entities in an application environment, attributes of objects and temporal relationships among objects, as well as object groupings and classifications (temporal and non-temporal) are all modeled as temporal objects. What distinguishes different kinds of (temporal) objects in a T-3DIS database is the set of structural and non-structural (temporal) relationships defined on them.

In addition to the three kinds of objects supported by the 3DIS, namely atomic [5], composite and type objects, the T-3DIS supports a fourth kind of object, namely *time-slice objects.*

Temporal *Composite* objects describe (non-atomic) entities and concepts of application environments. The information content of these objects can be interpreted meaningfully by the T-3DIS system through their decomposition into other objects. As such, there is a temporal constraint imposed on temporal objects which says that "a composite object exists at time T if each of its components exist at time t_i where $T > t_i$ and $i = 1, 2, ...$" [5].

An example of a temporal composite object is a student, e.g.,

$$\mathbf{Stud_1}([1989, 1990], 1).$$

The identifier $\mathbf{Stud_1}([1989, 1990], 1)$ is the system generated object-id that serves as the symbolic name (colloquially, the logical reference name) of this object. The composite object $\mathbf{Stud_1}([1989, 1990], 1)$ may be decomposed into a set of objects that define its characteristics, e.g., its social security number, name, status, advisor, etc. The first instant of the time interval of each of these objects must be less than the time interval of the object $Stud_1$. This implies that the object $Stud_1$ cannot exist *before* a name is assigned to it.

Temporal *Mapping* objects are a special kind of temporal composite object. Mappings can in general model arbitrary **temporal** relations among two objects. They also model both single and multi-valued temporal relations, where a multi-valued mapping is defined from a domain element to a set of range elements. Every mapping is defined in terms of, and may be decomposed into a domain type object, a range type object, the time that the relationship was established, the time that the relationship was disestablished (if the relationship is current then this value is set to ∞), the version in which the relationship was in effect, an inverse mapping object, the minimum number of values it may return, and the maximum number of values it may return.

Type objects specify the descriptive and classification information in a database. A type object is a structural specification of a group of atomic or composite objects. It denotes a collection of database objects, called its *members*, together with the shared common information about these members in terms of each object's Universal Object Identity [5]. The time of creation of each member of

---

[5] Atomic Objects objects are simple, nondecomposable "printables" and are treated in the T-3DIS the same as they are in the 3DIS.

a type object as well as its lifespan might be different. A type object is defined
in terms of its members, a set of mappings common to its members, called
member-mappings, the universal object identity of its members, the fundamental
semantic relationships between this type object and other type objects for several
discrete time points, the fundamental temporal relationships between this type
object and other time-slice objects for several discrete time points, and a set of
operations defined on its members.

Type objects do not specify the *temporal* specification of a group of objects.
If we were to allow them to do so, we would be facing tremendous difficulties
in not only determining the lifespans of objects but also their temporal interrelationships. More importantly we would also have introduced several temporal
semantic conflicts. For this reason, we have introduced a new kind of object
called a *time-slice object*. *Time-slice* objects specify the temporal and behavioral
information in a database for a *single discrete time point* t_i. They encapsulate
the Possible Object World of objects [5]. So in a *very* abstract sense, a collection
of time-slice objects will derive the corresponding type as shown in [5]. A member
of a time-slice object can belong to several time-slice objects; thus objects can
exist at different discrete time points. A time-slice object is defined in terms
of its members, a certain discrete time point that its members are active, the
possible object world of its members, a set of temporal mappings common to
its members, the fundamental relationships between time-slice objects and type
objects, the fundamental relationships between time-slice objects and other time-
slice objects, and a set of operations defined on its members.

Temporal Abstraction Mechanisms Basic associations among objects in T-
3DIS databases are established through a set of predefined abstraction primitives as well as the definition of additional abstraction primitives. As with the
3DIS, in the T-3DIS basic mappings support the definition of the three abstraction primitives of classification/instantiation, aggregation/decomposition, and
generalization/specialization. Here, we describe an additional set of predefined
temporal abstraction mechanisms particularly tailored for T-3DIS.

The fundamental associations among data and temporal data are captured
through a set of *basic temporal relationships* defined on objects, in addition to
the ones defined for the 3DIS. Basic temporal mappings support the definition
of the following abstraction primitives:

- **Temporal Assignment** is represented by *temporal version/member* mappings that each relates a temporal object such as an atomic or composite to
  a temporal version.
- **Temporalization** is represented by *type/time-slice* mappings that each relates a type object.
- **Temporal Uncertainty** is represented by *member/member* mappings that
  each relates with some degree of uncertainty a temporal object to another
  temporal object.
- **POW-to-POW identification** is represented by a possible object world/

possible object world mapping and facilitates the evolution of an object from one possible POW to another.

Temporal mappings also support the definition of operations common to the members of a type object and a time-slice object, namely their temporal constraint-evaluators. There is a difference between the 3DIS and T-3DIS when it comes to constraint-evaluators. While in the first case only true messages are allowed, and any checks on such messages are made at the time the message is input, in T-3DIS any message could potentially be true. Therefore, our model's constraints categorize information into true, false and meaningful the later making the specification of such constraints complicated. Also in the T-3DIS there is a set of primitive semantic constraints such as *always, sometimes, before, during, separately, contains* and *consecutive*. Even though in we introduce some temporal constraints, in this paper we primarily concentrate on the general features of the T-3DIS.

3.4 Temporal Specification Operations

A set of simple but functionally powerful temporal primitives, also called the T-3DIS *temporal specification* operations, is defined for the T-3DIS that supports the basic data definition and data manipulation temporal operations. The term **temporal operation** is loosely used to refer to a temporal action, i.e. a temporal operation, function or message. As with the 3DIS, these primitives are assumed to be embedded within a host programming language.

These operations allow users to add new temporal objects that may be of kind atomic, composite, type or time-slice. Unlike the 3DIS, but in the spirit of temporal databases, the T-3DIS does not allow an object to be deleted from the database. It is either suspended indefinitely or archived which is similar to a "virtual" delete. The operations allow users to also retrieve temporal inter-object relationships, to invoke behavioral objects, and to display objects on appropriate devices. [6]

- **CREATE : object-id**. The CREATE operation generates a new type object, adds it to the database, and returns its system generated object-id.
- **ATTACH-UOI(o:object,UOI):(UOI)**. This operation generates the universal object identity of an object. There is also a corresponding objects (it is possible to attach more than a single possible object world to a given object)
- **DEFINE**((o:object,temporal version) : (object-id,temporal version)). The define operation of the 3DIS is extended so as to generate a new atomic object and its temporal version and adds it to the database.
- **RELATE**(d:(oi ,tv),m:(oi ,tv),r:(oi,tv)) where oi and tv correspond to an object id and temporal version respectively. This operation generates a temporal relationship among objects and adds it to the database, where d is the

---

[6] The operations presented here are by no means exhaustive. Here we are presenting a flavor of the temporal operations supported by the T-3DIS.

domain-element, m is the mapping-element, and r is the range-element in the relationship. The arguments d, m, and r must have been CREATED, or DEFINED before this operation.

- **UNRELATE**(d:(oi,tv), m:(oi,tv), r:(oi,tv)). This operation destroys the specified temporal relationship from the database. If the specified relationship in an UNRELATE operation does not exist in the database, then this operation has no effect. Because T-3DIS is a temporal database, the operation

$$\text{UNRELATE(Mary}([1970, 1990], 1),$$
$$\text{Is}([1989, 1990], 1),$$
$$\text{GRAD}([1989, 1990], 2)).$$

does not destroy the relationship. Instead the temporal relationship "Is" is simply converted to its equivalent past temporal relationship "Was" and leaves the objects **Mary, Is,** and **GRAD** intact as follows:

$$\text{UNRELATE(Mary}([1970, 1990], 1),$$
$$\text{Was}([1989, 1990], 1),$$
$$\text{GRAD}([1989, 1990], 2)).$$

- **ARCHIVE**(i:object-id,temporal version). In view of the desire to maintained and accessible temporal information our model does not allow any deletions and in consequence, we are faced with an ever-growing storage size. To "eliminate" some of the side affects of this requirement, we have developed this operation to replace the "delete" operation of the 3DIS. It can be viewed as a "virtual" delete.

Tailored Temporal Operations The following operations are specifically tailored for the T-3DIS. In the following, D denotes d:(object-id,temporal version), M denotes m:(object-id,temporal version), and R denotes r:(object-id,temporal version). If the operation does not require a temporal version, the temporal version is assumed to be $[(0,0),0]$.

- **HISTORY**(D, M) : (t:dates) generates the history of an object.
- **PAST**(D, M) : ({ $\mathcal{R}_i, ..., \mathcal{R}_n$ }) generates the entire past of an object.
- **NEXT**(D, M, R) : ({ $\mathcal{R}_i, ..., \mathcal{R}_n$ }) generates the history of an object that immediately follows the current history.
- **DURING**(D) : ({ $\mathcal{D}_i, ..., \mathcal{D}_n$ }) generates a set of objects whose lifespan meets the lifespan of the given object.
- **OVERLAPS**(D) : ({ $\mathcal{D}_i, ..., \mathcal{D}_n$ }) generates a set of objects whose lifespan overlaps the lifespan of the given object.
- **MEETS**(D) : ({ $\mathcal{D}_i, ..., \mathcal{D}_n$ }) generates a set of objects whose lifespan meets the lifespan of the given object.
- **BEFORE**(D) : ({ $\mathcal{D}_i, ..., \mathcal{D}_n$ }) generates a set of objects whose lifespan is before the lifespan of the given object.

Along the same lines we have designed several other temporal operations such as for the historical mappings described [7].

3.5 The Geometric Representation Space

In extending the 3DIS to support temporal data, one of our main objectives was to preserve the 3DIS's 3-dimensional (3-D) framework that organizes database objects and their temporal interrelationships graphically. The geometric representation space is discrete, orthogonal, and is assumed to be located in the positive octant of a 3-D space. The three axes in the space represent the temporal domain, mapping and range axes. As with the 3DIS, all temporal database objects appear on both D and R axes, but the M-axis holds temporal mapping objects (a subset of all objects) only. Temporal relationships among objects are represented by specific, explicit points in this geometric space (termed "on" points) that are defined via their three coordinates, namely "(domain-object($[t_i, t_j], v$), mapping-object($[t_k, t_l], v$), range-object($[t_m, t_n], v$))" triples.

4 Concluding Remarks

In this paper we have shown how our temporal modeling elements and primitive operations can be used to augment the data modeling power of existing object models. To do this, we have described an approach to the design and development a model that integrates time with the 3DIS and provides (temporal) meaning to objects. Our work presents a first step towards the synthesis of an integrated object data model that supports the temporal aspects of data modeling in addition to the structural and dynamic ones. We expect the mechanisms developed in this paper, to have a direct impact on how various temporal properties of objects can be incorporated into yet other existing object models.

5 Acknowledgements

The authors are highly thankful to the editors for enumerating the changes needed to improve this paper, and to Ken Been for making suggestions on the final draft of the paper.

References

1. H. Afsarmanesh and D. McLeod. The 3DIS: An extensible, object-oriented information management environment. *ACM Transactions on Information Systems*, 7(4):339–377, October 1990.
2. J. A. Jr. Bubenko. The temporal dimension in information modeling. In *Architecture and Models in Data Base Management Systems*. North-Holland, 1977.
3. R. Elmasri and S. Navathe. *Fundamentals of Database Systems*. Benjamin/Cummings, 1989.
4. S. K. Gadia and C. Yeung. A generalized model for a temporal relational database. In *Proceedings of the ACM SIGMOD International Conference on Management of Data*. ACM SIGMOD, 1988.

5. N. Pissinou. A conceptual framework for time in object databases. Technical Report CRI-90-26, Computer Research Institute, University of Southern California, Los Angeles CA, 1990.

6. N. Pissinou. Extending the 3DIS to support time. Technical Report CRI-91-1, Computer Research Institute, University of Southern California, Los Angeles CA, 1991.

7. N. Pissinou. *Time in Object Databases*. PhD thesis, University of Southern California, Los Angeles, California, December 1991.

Inductive Dependencies and Approximate Databases

Debby Keen and Arcot Rajasekar

Department of Computer Science, University of Kentucky, Lexington, KY 40506

Abstract. Query processing in a (relational) database context has been mainly confined to deducing information that is available in the database. The answers given to queries are supported by available data in the database and are computed using the classical operations of select, project and join. When the query cannot be answered using the above operations the database system returns an empty answer. But there are cases where an approximate answer for the query would be desirable instead of no answer from the database. In this paper, we provide one such approximation technique, inductive dependencies, that can be used to enhance conventional relational databases. The approach finds an approximation for a null value in the database, by using similarities, aggregate functions and relationships that are not expressible by functional dependencies. Inductive dependencies can also be applied to heterogeneous databases, where relationships between databases need to be expressed in a concise way.

1 Introduction

Query processing in a (relational) database context has been mainly confined to deducing information that is available in the database. That is, the answers given to queries are supported by available data in the database and are computed using the classical operations of select, project and join. When the query cannot be answered using the above operations the database system returns an empty answer.

But when it is not possible to deduce an answer to a query from a tuple, it would be worthwhile to provide an approximate answer using information which is *similar* to the one from which the query would be answered. In this paper, we provide one such approximation technique, based on data dependencies, that can be adapted for relational databases. The approach we develop is based on extrapolation or induction and provides an approximate answer to a query using available related information from the database.

Considerable research has been reported in the areas of incomplete information [2, 5, 13, 14, 15, 17] and functional dependencies [6, 1, 21, 8]. The area of incomplete information deals with representation and processing of attribute values in a relational table, which are 'missing' or *null* (that is, values at present unknown). Functional dependencies provide semantic information about the rigid relationships between attributes in relational tables. Functional dependencies have been used to provide answers even with null values and to fill out incomplete information. Work reported in [12, 22] shows the use of functional dependencies in supplementing incomplete information.

In this paper we consider a different method for computing the value of a null entry in a relational table. We contend that, similar to the rigid dependencies provided by functional dependencies, one can define approximate dependencies which provide a semantics that can be used to compute values of a null entry. The method can be illustrated as follows. Consider that someone is checking to see if a particular stock was up or down at today's opening of the market. Assume that the stock information database does not contain the desired information. But there is information regarding other stocks that are "similar" that indicates they are all "down". This data can be used to provide an approximate answer for our original query. It is our contention that the inquirer would be happier with the approximate answer, "the stock you asked about is probably down", rather than with a null answer for the query.

There are many such situations where humans use available information to provide an approximate answer about a missing item. In this paper we explore methods to precisely define inductive approaches that can be used by a relational database system to provide approximate answers. We define what are called inductive dependencies and show how query answering procedures can use inductive dependencies to provide approximate answers when complete data is unavailable. In the example discussed above, we made use of an inductive dependency which can be loosely stated as follows: "The direction of change of a particular stock inductively depends upon the direction of change of the other stocks in the same category." We made use of this inductive dependency to answer the query which otherwise has no derivable answer from the database. There are problems associated with dealing with inductive reasoning such as the confidence of the approximate answer given. We provide syntax and semantics for inductive dependencies which address such problems.

A practical need for inductive dependencies can be justified as follows: even though for some sets of data it is not possible to provide a strict dependency, it may be possible to provide a looser dependency among the data. Such types of information are very often used in statistics and probability theory to provide approximate answers to queries for which there are no precise answers. Inductive dependencies make these notions user-definable and precise. Consider the following relationships for which one cannot write any rigid dependency criterion:

1. The salaries of assistant managers with similar experience are similar.
2. Similar houses in the same locality cost the same amount.
3. A materials research database may have null values for materials that have not been investigated yet. These values may be approximated by comparing the properties to those of known similar materials.
4. A family generally shares the same surname, but this is not a true functional dependency, due to remarriages, etc. If a census database included the members of a family but some last names were missing, they could be inferred by using the head of household's last name.

The above 'rules of thumb' are not inflexible dependencies which can be en-

forced in a database nor are they rules which can be used to provide precise answers from a database. But they are rules which can provide approximate answers which are often sufficient for human uses. We formalize methods for providing such approximate answers in this paper. Inductive dependencies are unusual in that they are flexible enough to be used in many different areas, from null values to heterogeneous databases, just about anywhere a "heuristic" rule is needed.

Section 2 provides the required terminology, sections 3 and 4 formulate the theory of inductive views. Section 5 develops additional uses for the inductive formalism. Section 6 discusses some of the properties of inductive dependencies. Section 7 discusses some advantages and disadvantages of inductive dependencies. Section 8 provides a comparison with other approaches.

2 Terminology

Let U be a nonempty finite set of symbols, called *attributes*. A *relation scheme* is a nonempty subset of U. A *database scheme*, D, is a nonempty set of relation schemes. For each attribute A, there is a set called the *domain* of A. We also include a special symbol, ?, called the null value as part of the domain of each attribute in U. A *tuple* over a relation scheme R is a mapping that, for each attribute $A \in R$, associates an element of A's domain with A. A *relation state* over a relation scheme R is a finite set of tuples over R. We use r to denote a relation state over R. A *database state* over a database scheme D is a set of relation states over D's relation schemes. We use D to denote a database scheme over D. Given a relation scheme R, a subset of attributes of R, say X, is a *key* to R, if X uniquely identifies each tuple in a relation state r of R. That is, no two tuples agree on all attributes of a key.

If t is a tuple in a relation state r over scheme R and $X \subseteq R$, $t[X]$ is the restriction of the mapping to X, and the *projection* of r, a relational state of R, onto X is the set $\{t[X] : t \in r\}$. Let r and s be relation states over R and S respectively. The selection of a set of tuples from relation r, $\sigma_F r$, is the set of tuples in r which satisfies the formula F. The formula F, is a boolean formula, and is defined using attributes and domain values which are connected with logical and arithmetic comparison operators. The Cartesian product of r and s is $r \times s = \{t : t$ a tuple over $R \cup S$, and $t[R] \in r, t[S] \in s\}$. The join of r and $s, r \bowtie_F s$, is set of tuples in the Cartesian product of r and s which satisfy the formula F. The formula F, is of the form $i\theta j$ where i is an attribute in r and j is an attribute in s and θ is a logical or arithmetic comparison operator. We consider that the null value symbol, ?, does not take part in any of the above operations. [14] provides definitions of these operators on tables with null values. The reader is referred to [21] for additional details on the terminology used in the paper. Next we define functional dependencies between attributes of a relation.

Definition 1. [21]

Let $R(A_1, A_2, \ldots, A_n)$ be a relation scheme, and let X and Y be subsets of

$\{A_1, A_2, \ldots, A_n\}$ We say $X \to Y$, read "X functionally determines Y" or "Y functionally depends upon X", if whatever relation r is the current value for **R**, it is not possible that r has two tuples that agree in the components for all attributes in the set X yet disagree in one or more components for attributes in the set Y. □

3 Inductive Dependencies

Inductive dependencies provide supplemental or approximate information about data in a relational database.

Definition 2. Let $\mathbf{R}(A_1, A_2, \ldots, A_n)$ be a relation scheme, and let X be a (possibly null) subset of $\{A_1, A_2, \ldots, A_n\}$ and Y be an element in $\{A_1, A_2, \ldots, A_n\}$ such that Y is not in X. We say $X \hookrightarrow Y$, read "X inductively determines Y" or "Y inductively depends upon X", if whatever relation r is the current value for **R**, and if r has a set of tuples, r', which agree in the components for all attributes in the set X, then any null (or undefined) value for Y in any tuple in r' can be approximately determined (using an approximation function) from the non-null values of attribute Y in r'. The set of tuples in r' which have non-null values for attribute Y is called an *inductive determinant*. □

Example 1. Let the relation $\mathbf{R}(category, stockname, price fluctuation)$ be part of an database which provides data regarding stocks traded on the New York Stock Exchange. One can identify an inductive dependency which says that *the price fluctuation of a stock can be inductively determined from other stocks which are in the same category*. This information can be used to provide an approximate answer when no price fluctuation data is available for a particular stock. The inductive dependency can be encoded as $category \hookrightarrow price fluctuation$. □

In concept, inductive dependencies are similar to functional dependencies, but inductive dependencies define approximate relationships, whereas the functional dependencies provide rigid connections. They are "orthogonal" to each other. That is, functional dependencies can be seen as providing data dependency information in a horizontal direction (along the rows of relations) whereas inductive dependencies can be seen as having an additional component in the vertical direction (along the columns of a relation). Intuitively, if a tuple in a relation has an undefined value in a column, then an approximate value can be computed from a *subset of values* present in that column in the relation. An inductive dependency provides a means to generate the table which contains the subset of values in the column.

Once an inductive determinant is generated, by using an inductive dependency $X \hookrightarrow Y$, then the column of attribute Y can be projected and used in computing an approximate value. Next we define an approximation function which can be used to compute this value.

Definition 3. An *approximation function* is a function which takes a single column relation and returns a single value or a set of values. An approximation function is either an aggregate function which returns the average, maximum, minimum, median, or the mode (the most repeated value in the column) which returns a single value from the domain of X, or, an identity function which returns a set of values from the domain of X, which is equal to the relation itself, but not containing any multiple occurrences. The function ignores null entries in the input relation. □

In the case of a relation with a non-numeric domain, approximation functions such as the median, maximum, minimum and average would not be applicable, but the other two functions listed in the above definition, mode and identity, would be useful.

Inductive dependencies are used as follows. Assume that given a value for attributes X one wants to find an approximate value for attribute Y in a relation state r of scheme R. We first make the following assumptions. One, X is a key and two, the Y value is undefined for that X value. The assumption of X being a key is made so that X is non-null and uniquely determines a tuple. (Actually, the assumption that the tuple be uniquely determined can be relaxed, but we retain the assumption to simplify our procedure.) Let t be the tuple given by the value for attribute X. Let $Z \hookrightarrow Y$ be an inductive dependency in R. Let z be the value for attribute Z in tuple t. Again we assume that z is non-null, otherwise we will not be able to apply the inductive criterion. Next, we select all tuples in r which have $Z = z$. This set of tuples, say r', forms the inductive determinant. The Y attribute is next projected and given as input to an approximation function. The value returned by the function provides an approximate answer for the query. The following procedure is based on this approach:

Procedure 1 : $\mathrm{Proc1}(r,x,i,f,Y,y)$
Input: r, x, i, f, Y **Output:** y
     r: relation state with attribute Y and non-empty sets of attributes X and Z
     x: value for attributes X (Key)
     Y: attribute name for which a value is being queried
     y: value for attribute Y (undefined in r)
     f: approximation function to be used
     i: an inductive dependency $Z \hookrightarrow Y$
Step 1: $z = \Pi_z(\sigma_{X=x} r)$
Step 2: If z has null value return fail
Step 3: $r' = \sigma_{z=z} r$
Step 4: $r'' = \Pi_Y r'$
Step 5: $y = f(r'')$ □

Example 2. Consider the following database of stock exchange information (Relation R_1).

Relation R_1

Category	Stock Name	Fluctuation
Energy	Brit.Pet	+2.5
Food	P&G	+3.9
Energy	Standard	+4.3
Industr.	Beth. Steel	-3.1
Energy	Mobile	-2.7
Industr.	Chrysler	+9.8
Food	Kelloggs	?
Energy	Sun Power	+4.7
HiTech	Apple	-4.5
Energy	Royal Oil	?

Assume that there is an inductive dependency, $Z \hookrightarrow Y$ where $Z = \{Category\}$ and $Y = Fluctuation$. That is, the amount of change is inductively dependent on the category that the stock is in. Consider that we need to answer the query: *What is the fluctuation for Royal Oil?* ¿From R_1, we cannot deduce this information as it is unavailable. But using the induction dependence of Y on Z, we can find an approximate answer. Since Z inductively determines the value for Y, we first find the value of Z when *Stock Name = Royal Oil* (Step 1). This is deduced from R_1 as $Z = \{Energy\}$ Next we generate the inductive determinant for this value of Z (Relation R_2) (Step 2).

Relation R_2

Category	Stock Name	Fluctuation
Energy	Brit.Pet	+2.5
Energy	Standard	+4.3
Energy	Mobile	-2.7
Energy	Sun Power	+4.7
Energy	Royal Oil	?

Now, we can use any approximation function on the column *Fluctuation* in R_2 (Steps 3 and 4). Assume that we use the averaging function, then we get

Fluctuation for Royal Oil = +2.2. □

When more than one inductive dependency has been defined the following procedure can be used. In the next section we consider other ways of dealing with multiple inductive dependencies.

Procedure 2 Proc2(r,x,f,f',Y,y)
  Input: r, x, f, f', Y **Output:** y
    r, x, f, y, Y: *as defined in Procedure* Proc1
    f': *global approximation function to be used*
Step 1: For each inductive dependency (for any Z) $i = Z \hookrightarrow Y$,
      do-begin
        Proc1(r,x,i,f,Y)
        Collect the values of Y in relation r'
      do-end
Step 2: $y = f'(r')$ □

Two functions, f and f' are used in Procedure *Proc2*, so that the answers generated by all relevant inductive dependencies can be combined flexibly. For example, f can be a 'maximum' function and f' can be a minimum function, and the answer generated will be a least upper bound on the values generated by the inductive dependencies.

The concept of induction is very general and dependencies based on induction can be used in more than one way. Different types of induction-based dependencies can be defined. Next, we show the versatility of the inductive approach by discussing a different use of inductive dependencies.

Consider queries of the form "Is $X = x$ and $Y = y$ supported by the database?" Assume that there is an inductive dependence $X \hookrightarrow Y$. In such cases the probability of Y taking the value y, when $X = x$, can be estimated using an inductive dependency and a probability function. In the following definition, if r is a relation table, then by $|r|$ we mean the number of tuples in r.

Definition 4. A *probability function* is a function which takes a single column relation $r(X)$ and a value x in the domain of X, and returns a numeric value between 0 and 1 computed as the ratio of the number of tuples in $\sigma_{X=x}r(X)$ to the number of tuples in $r(X)$. The function is written as follows:
$$f_p(r(X), x) = \frac{|\sigma_{X=x}r(X)|}{|r(X)|} \qquad \qquad \Box$$

The computation is described by the following procedure.

Procedure 3 Proc3(r,x,y,i,p)
  Input: r, x, y **Output:** p
    r: *relation state*
    x: *value for attributes X (Key)*
    y: *value for attribute Y*
    i: *an inductive dependency* $Z \hookrightarrow Y$
    p: *probability that Y takes value y when X has value x*
  Step 1: $z = \Pi_z(\sigma_{X=x}r)$
  Step 2: If z has null value return fail
  Step 3: $r' = \sigma_{z=z}r$
  Step 4: $r'' = \Pi_Y r'$
  Step 5: $p = f_p(r'', y)$ $\Box$

Note the similarity between Procedures *Proc1* and *Proc3*. We also define a new type of dependency called proportional dependency in Section 5.

4   Inductive Rules

There are two problems which need to be considered before one can apply the inductive criterion. First, there may be more than one definition for the notion of similarity for finding answers for a particular attribute. For example, similarities between houses can be defined in different ways. This leads to problems such as which particular criterion is better than others or which particular criterion is applicable in a database instance. This also leads to the problem that if two criteria provide answers which are different, then how should the two answers be interpreted. A solution to the problem is to provide a *static confidence factor*, C_c, (on a scale of 0 to 1) of a particular criterion. When the user (or database manager) defines a set of inductive dependencies for a particular attribute, he/she should also provide an ordering of their relative importance. For example, the inductive dependency $\{age, size\} \hookrightarrow price$ may have a higher C_c value than that of an inductive dependency like $\{type, size\} \hookrightarrow price$. On such a scale, a functional dependency will have a confidence factor of 1.

The second problem is that even if an inductive criterion is definable for a particular attribute in a database scheme, the answer which is estimated from a database instance may be a poor approximation. For example, consider that there is only one house whose price is listed and which corresponds to the similarity definition for a house we are querying. The answer that is estimated from this database is of less value compared to the answer generated from another database which has 20 entries for similar houses. A solution for this problem is to provide a *dynamic confidence factor*, C_i, (on a scale of 0 to 1) based on the instance of the database from which it is computed. A dynamic confidence factor may be defined using information such as the standard deviation of the values in the inductive determinant table and the size of the table.

We combine the definitions of inductive dependencies given in Definition 2 along with the notions of confidence factors to provide "inductive rules", which can be written by a user or the database manager as follows:

$X < action, C_i, C_c > \hookrightarrow < guardconditions > Y$

C_i is the dynamic confidence factor; C_c is the static confidence factor. Guard conditions are used to select a subset of tuples from the inductive determinant. (As given in Definition 2, X is used to form the set called the inductive determinant.) These selected tuples are then used to actually compute the value of Y. If no guard condition is given then the full inductive determinant is used. Guard conditions are made of Boolean formulas as defined in Section 1, involving any attribute in relation r, such as Y-value > 5. Operations on system variables/functions such as "time of day" can also be used and prove very useful for time-sensitive constraints, as "tuples with timestamps greater than 8 seconds before now". Guard conditions can be seen as providing a more restricted definition for "similar" compared to inductive determinants.

The action, or approximation function, defines what to do with the tuples that are selected by the dependency as being "similar" and then possibly reduced further by the guard conditions. Statistical functions like mode or mean may be used for the approximation function. User defined functions may also be used to check to see if a tuple has a certain property before including it in the computations for the result. The identity function can be used to pass the values through unchanged to the user, or to a global approximation function.

Next we provide an example to show the flavour of how the confidence factors can be used.

Example 3. In Example 2, if the query had been *What is the price fluctuation for Kelloggs?*, the *Category* for the inductive dependency *Category* $\hookrightarrow$ *Fluctuation* would be *Food*. Then the inductive determinant for the query would have only one tuple with a non-null value for the attribute *Fluctuation*. This situation would have a much lower dynamic confidence factor than the one in Example 2, where there was more data to use in the calculation of the missing value. A dynamic confidence factor $C_i = \frac{sizeof determinant}{sizeof fulltable}$ will give $C_i = 0.5$ for an answer about *Royal Oil* and $C_i = 0.1$ for an answer about *Kelloggs* computed using this table.

For the inductive dependency in Example 2 we can associate a static confidence factor depending upon the table of data to which it is applied. We can place a high confidence value for an answer if the table of data was gathered from the official New York Stock Exchange reports. On the other hand, we can attribute a lower value of C_c if the table of data had been concerning "penny stocks" which are wildly volatile.

5 Proportional Inductive Dependencies

In Section 3, we saw inductive dependencies, which provided a direct dependency between a null value and values which have a common determiner. But in some cases, it may be possible that a simple dependency may not hold, but a complex inductive method might be needed. In this section, we study one such inductive approach, called proportional inductive dependence. We illustrate the approach with an example.

Example 4. Assume that we are intending to buy an item *I3*. We find that the particular item is available in shop *S1* but unavailable in shop *S2* and we know that shop *S2* sells items at a cheaper rate compared to shop *S1*. We come to know that shop *S2* might get the item in a week and we wish to find out the price of *I3* in shop *S2* to figure out if it is worth waiting for the item to become available in *S2*. Assume that the store manager at *S2* is not able (or willing) to provide a price for *I3*. In such a case we can use an approach as follows: We find prices for items which are similar to *I3* (say items *I1* and *I2*) which are available in both shops and compare their respective prices. Using the average ratio of prices for the items in the two shops we can proportionately compute an approximate value of item *I3* if sold in shop *S2*. The computed price can be used to figure if the difference in price is worth waiting for a week. The calculation can be done as illustrated using the following table of information (Relation R_5).

Relation R_5

Seller	Item	Price
S1	I1	21
S1	I2	43
S1	I3	65
S2	I1	15
S2	I2	32
S2	I3	?

Ratio of price of item $I1$ in shop $S1$ and $S2 = 21/15 = 1.4$
Ratio of price of item $I2$ in shop $S1$ and $S2 = 43/32 = 1.34$
Average ratio of prices of items in shop $S1$ and $S2 = average(1.4, 1.34) = 1.37$
Using this ratio, the price of item $I3$ in store $S2 = 65/1.37 = 47.4$ □

The averaging done in the above example can be replaced by other approximation functions such as minimum, maximum or the mode value. Again, in the above example, if one can get prices for the items from another store (say $S3$), then an approximation function can be used to obtain an estimation for the price of item $I3$ in store $S2$ based on price ratios computed for stores $S1$ and $S2$, and for stores $S3$ and $S2$. Moreover, the larger the number of prices of items we compare and the larger the number of stores we use in our computation, the better will be our approximate value computed using this method. Next, we make precise this notion of proportional inductive computation.

Definition 5. Let $R(A_1, A_2, \ldots, A_n)$ be a relation scheme, and let X and Y be distinct subsets of $\{A_1, A_2, \ldots, A_n\}$ such that $\{X, Y\}$ forms a key for R. Let Z be an element in $\{A_1, A_2, \ldots, A_n\}$ such that Z is not in X or Y. We say $< X; Y >\rightsquigarrow Z$, read "Given X, Y proportionately determines Z" or "Z proportionately depends upon Y given X", if whatever relation r is the current value for R, and if r has two sets of tuples, r' and r'' (with associated relations R' and R''), where each tuple in r' (resp. r'') agree on the value of X, then any null (or undefined) value for Z in any tuple in r can be approximately determined (using a proportionality function) from the non-null values of attributes $Z_{r'}$ and $Z_{r''}$ in r''', where The set of tuples in r''' is called a *proportional determinant*. □

Definition 6. A *proportionality function* is a function which takes a double column relation $r(X, Y)$ and returns a single value or a set of values. First, one more column is added to the relation state $r(X, Y)$ to get $r'(X, Y, Z)$ where the value of Z in each tuple in r' is given by the ratio of the X and Y values in the tuple. Next, column Z in r' is projected and is given as an input to an approximation function which returns a single value or a set of values as its output. □

A procedure similar to Procedure *Proc1* for using proportional dependencies can be defined [19]. Proportional inductive rules can be defined in a manner similar to that of inductives dependencies given in Section 4.

6 Properties of Inductive Dependencies

In this section, we look at some of the properties for inductive dependencies. In the case of functional dependencies, Armstrong's axioms [1] are used to compute the complete set of functional dependencies implied by a given set of functional dependencies.

The following axioms, similar to Armstrong's axioms and their extensions, can be defined for inductive dependencies.

Definition 7. Let R (resp. D) be a relation (resp. database) scheme.
Let $W, X, Y, Z \in U$ where U is the attribute list of R (resp. D).
1. **Reflexivity**: If $Y \subseteq X$, then $X \hookrightarrow Y$
2. **Augmentation**: If $Z \subseteq W$ and $X \hookrightarrow Y$, then $XW \hookrightarrow YZ$
3. **Transitivity**: If $X \hookrightarrow Y$ and $Y \hookrightarrow Z$, then $Y \hookrightarrow Z$
4. **Pseudotransitivity**: Let W be null-free. If $X \hookrightarrow Y$ and $YW \hookrightarrow Z$ then $XW \hookrightarrow Z$
5. **Union**: If $X \hookrightarrow Y$ and $X \hookrightarrow Z$ then $X \hookrightarrow YZ$
6. **Decomposition**: If $X \hookrightarrow YZ$, then $X \hookrightarrow Y$ and $X \hookrightarrow Z$

The question arises if the above axioms are obeyed by inductive dependencies. The answer is that not all inductive dependencies obey them, but, by putting restrictions on schemas and inductive dependencies, one can show that the restricted database obeys the axioms. One such restriction, called independent inductive dependencies, [19] can be defined as follows:

Definition 8. Let $D = \{R_1, \ldots, R_n\}$ be a database scheme.
Let $ID = \{ID_1, \ldots, ID_m\}$ be a set of inductive dependencies for D. ID is called *independent* with respect to D if each $R_i = \{X_i, Y_i\}$ where $X_i \hookrightarrow Y_i$ is an inductive dependency in ID.

The following theorem shows that for a restricted class of independent inductive dependencies the axioms in Definition 8 are sound and complete.

Theorem 9. *[19] Let D be a database scheme and ID be a set of inductive dependencies for D such that ID is independent with respect to D. Then Axioms 1-6 hold for ID.*

Another set of properties that need to be studied, is the interaction between functional dependencies and inductive dependencies. First, functional dependencies are a special form of inductive dependencies. When $X \rightarrow Y$ is an functional dependency then $X \hookrightarrow Y$ is an inductive dependency. Applying the inductive dependency yields the same result as applying the functional dependency when finding the null for a tuple in which the Y attribute is undefined. We can also prove a strong result showing that there is a transitive relationship between a functional dependency and an inductive dependency, when the inductive dependency is applied using the identity function.

Theorem 10. *Let $\mathbf{R}$ be a relational scheme. Let W, X, Y, Z be subsets of $\mathbf{R}$. Assume that we use identity function as the approximation function while computing inductive dependencies. Then,*
(1) If $X \rightarrow Y$ and $Y \hookrightarrow Z$ then $X \hookrightarrow Z$
(2) If $X \hookrightarrow Y$ and $Y \rightarrow Z$ then $X \hookrightarrow Z$
(3) If $X \rightarrow Y$ and $YW \hookrightarrow Z$ then $XW \hookrightarrow Z$
(4) If $X \hookrightarrow Y$ and $YW \rightarrow Z$ then $XW \hookrightarrow Z$ □

In relational databases, the notion of a key plays the part of identifying a unique tuple in an instance of a relation. Functional dependences provide a method to identify the keys of a relation.

It is not possible to use inductive dependencies to identify a key in a relation. But an analogous notion of a null-extended key can be defined using inductive dependencies.

Definition 11. Let $\mathbf{R}(A_1, A_2, \ldots, A_n)$ be a relation scheme, and let X be a non-empty subset of $\{A_1, A_2, \ldots, A_n\}$. Let r be the relation that is the current value of R. X is a *null-extended key (n-key)* if X is non-null in r and X is a determinant for all attributes not in X.

In the case of independent inductive dependencies, we can use the algorithm for finding the closure of attribute sets to find null-extended keys for a relation.

In fact, the more attributes are used in the head of the inductive dependency, the more information can be considered to decide which tuples are "similar" to the one in question. This should lead to better answers to queries. Intuitively, the more you know about a relationship, the better your approximation will be. The following lemma shows that the size of the determinant decreases as the length of an n-key increases.

In the case of superkeys, addition of attributes to the superkey yields another superkey. But in the case of a null-extended key, this property does not hold, as shown by Lemma 1.

Lemma 12. *Let $R(A_1, A_2, \ldots, A_n)$ be a relation scheme, and let X be a non-empty subset of $\{A_1, A_2, \ldots, A_n\}$ and let Y be a non-empty proper subset of X.*

If $Y \hookrightarrow A_i$ and $X \hookrightarrow A_i$ are two inductive dependencies for R, then $X_d \subseteq Y_d$ where X_d and Y_d are the inductive determinants for $X \hookrightarrow A_i$ and $Y \hookrightarrow A_i$.

Proof:

Let relation r be the current value for R, and let t_1 be a tuple in r which has a null value for the attribute A_i. Let $Y_d = \{t | t[Y] = t_1[Y] \text{ and } t[A_i] \text{ is not null}\}$ and $X_d = \{t | t[X] = t_1[X] \text{ and } t[A_i] \text{ is not null}\}$.

We show that $X_d \subseteq Y_d$.

Assume $t \in X_d$. This means that $t[X] = t_1[X]$. Since $Y \subseteq X$, $t[Y] = t_1[Y]$. Hence, $t \in Y_d$, by the definition of Y_d.

Since, we are dealing with approximate functions, statistical analysis of inductive dependencies also become important. In particular when there is more than one inductive dependency that can be used to compute the value of unavailable data for a particular attribute, metrics for comparing the worth of each of the dependencies are needed. Next, we discuss such metrics for comparing two inductive dependencies and develop semantics as to which inductive dependency is a better approximation of the two.

Standard statistical analysis provides a tool to define properties of inductive dependencies [23]. This technique is useful when we are operating on numeric values. The standard statistical measures of *variability* as defined using *standard deviation* and *variance* provides a metric for finding the worth of an inductive dependency. Another important measure can be the number of values which are used in the computation. Standard formulas can be used in defining these measures. The size of the inductive determinant table or the proportional determinant table provides this measure. We consider that a meaningful measure of inductive dependence is given by the two-tuple < *Standard deviation, Size of determinant table*>. That is, the smaller the standard deviation and the larger the size of the determinant table, the better is the approximate value computed using the inductive dependency. This measure can be used to compare two (average) values computed using two inductive dependencies. These techniques can be used to define the dynamic confidence factors discussed in Section 4.

In the case of non-numeric values the statistical formulations of average, standard deviation and variance are not applicable. Instead we define a different measure of worth for an inductive dependency. In such case, the measure of inductive dependency can be given by the ratio of the number of different values in the Y-column of the inductive determinant to the number of tuples in the inductive determinant. The smaller the measure given by the ratio, the better will be the values given by an inductive dependency.

7 Advantages and Disadvantages

Inductive dependencies can cover situations where functional dependencies do not work, or work poorly, where the user needs more flexibility than a functional dependency can give. Inductive dependencies can be combined with functional dependencies to work "on top of" existing databases without modifications to the database schema.

Inductive dependencies are useful in situations where the data in a database is still evolving. The data may not be "settled" enough to make the functional dependencies obvious to the designer. Inductive dependencies can be thought of as "trial runs" for the functional dependencies that will be put in place when the database is complete. Inductive dependencies do not insist that all the tuples in the relation follow exactly the same function. The guard conditions can spell out the tuples that should be involved in an inductive dependency. Thus the tuples that do not pass the "guards" do not cause the inductive dependency to be rejected on *all* tuples. Inductive dependencies can include in the "guards" time limitations on which tuples to use, such as "use only tuples that have been updated in the last 5 minutes", or "use only tuples from this time period". This can reduce the amount of processing needed, as fewer tuples are selected.

The amount of processing to deal with an inductive dependency is on the same order as answering a query with a definite answer - the same size table is used for both. Hence using inductive dependencies does not increase the complexity of query processing.

Another area where inductive dependencies can be useful is heterogeneous databases or multidatabases. If data is repeated in more than one site, it can become inconsistent. An inductive dependency can be used to determine how to derive the "best" approximation in the face of inconsistency.

In a heterogeneous database, suppose one database has a relation $r1(Name, Gender, Dept)$, and another database has a relation $r2(Name, Dept)$.

Both relations are complete, i.e., no null values. These two relations need to be merged to support a view for a user who needs all three attributes. An inductive dependency can be used to "fill in the blanks" in relation $r2$. The simplest inductive dependency would specify that the missing attribute be filled in with a constant value, such as 'male'. Of course, more sophisticated methods could be used too, e.g., calculate the ratio of male persons to the total number of people and use the ratio as a dynamic certainty factor on the value 'male'.

The method of inductive dependencies, like any other, can be abused. If invalid assumptions are made when writing the inductive dependencies, then incorrect answers to queries can be produced. Some of this can be remedied by experience; as the user gains practice with using the inductive dependencies, the inductive dependencies can be improved and corrected. Also, results given using the inductive dependencies will be prefaced by an indication that this information is approximate; most inductive dependencies should contain some way to determine how reliable a result will be.

Multiple inductive dependencies pose another problem. Tuples can be judged by different kinds of "similarity", which can result in inductive dependencies giving two different answers. This can be remedied by describing the process behind both answers and letting the user choose which he wants, or by choosing which answer is "better" by a partial ordering of "quality" of answers. One answer could be considered better than another if it subsumes the other.

A problem that inductive dependencies cannot ameliorate is the amount of data available - if there is only a small amount of data, the results will not be as accurate (measured against the real world) as if there were more data available. A dynamic confidence factor will have an indication of this so that the user can take it into account.

One should be very careful not only when defining an inductive criterion but also when using it. That is, when misdefined or misused, it can give misleading answers. Operations such as transitivity and augmentation may not necessarily produce the intended answers. Hence the use of inductive dependencies should be done with care. But if properly defined and used, inductive dependencies will provide a richer set of answers compared to traditional database operations.

8   Comparisons with Other Methods

Hence the systems which use functional dependencies to answer incomplete databases [12, 22] can also use inductive dependencies. Imelinski [14] gives a thorough study of such incomplete databases. As noted earlier, inductive dependencies are generalized forms of functional dependencies and any method using functional dependencies can be generalized to handle inductive dependencies. Inductive dependencies are different from systems which provide default values for "null" values [7].

Inductive dependencies are not really like fuzzy logic [24]; they do not require the user to decide on the numerical value of "true", "some", etc. Inductive dependencies generate normal tuples, according to the database schema given, with no special markers or tags that have to be maintained, such as in the case of multi-valued logics [4], or "maybe tuples"[10].

Inductive dependencies are also different from methods that add metrics that measure the distance between the tuple with the unknown value and the other tuples in the database [18]. These can be quite complex for the user to use, requiring the establishing of scales to measure how far "yellow" is from "green", for example. These methods usually have to compute the "distance" in some space from the query or unknown value to all other tuples in the relation, at least. Inductive dependencies use only the tuples in the relation that are "similar" to the query or unknown value, and conditions in the guards are usually much simpler to formulate than arbitrary numeric scales.

Inductive dependencies used with a database are somewhat akin to a probabilistic database which attempts to use the "most likely" value for the attribute that has its value missing by the average or standard deviation of all the values in the domain of the attribute. This method is good when values are numeric or easily converted to numeric values. Otherwise the "most likely" value is obtained by counting, or the user is asked to set up a scale or metric. This is similar to some actions of a database with inductive dependencies. However, probabilistic databases tend to assume all domain values are known and equally likely (to simplify the calculations). Inductive dependencies use repeated values of an attribute to weight that value more heavily, using statistical functions, etc. The theory developed here shares properties with statistical databases [21].

Inductive dependencies are similar to some methods of handling data inconsistencies in multidatabase systems. When data retrieved about the same item from different locations disagrees, some means of deciding what to report to the user is necessary. These methods are similar to inductive dependencies in that they include a good deal of the semantics behind the data in deciding which data item (or combination of data items) to choose [20, 3]. Inductive dependencies, properly adapted, would provide another means of extracting information from heterogeneous databases, especially in cases where there is a disagreement.

Inductive dependencies have some roots in knowledge acquisition and reasoning. [9] Reasoning by analogy involves determining which objects or concepts are "similar" and relevant, so that an analogy can be applied. Inductive dependencies make much of this explicit by the fact of the dependency and by the guard conditions provided.

Of course, induction is an important tool in machine learning studies. Inductive dependencies apply induction by allowing the user to supply relationships that the user has learned. Inductive dependencies can be the end product of a machine learning cycle. [16]

9 Conclusion

We have discussed a new methodology which can be applied to compute missing information from a relational database. We showed how inductive knowledge which we use in everyday life can be precisely defined using inductive dependencies. We also defined procedures which can be applied to existing relational databases. Finally, we also discussed some properties of inductive dependencies. In this paper we extended functional dependencies, by relaxing the rigid constraint imposed by them. Similar techniques can be adapted when dealing with other kinds of dependencies such as multi-valued dependencies [11]. We are currently exploring these extensions. We are also looking at implementation issues for inductive rules as a user interface over a relational database scheme. We believe that dependencies based on inductive principles will increase the expressive power of databases and will be of utility when no direct answer is derivable from a database.

10 Acknowledgements

The first author would like to acknowledge support from Pikeville College, the Pew Foundation and the Faculty Scholars Program.

The second author acknowledges the support of the National Science Foundation under grant number CCR-9110721.

References

1. W.W. Armstrong. Dependency Structures of Database Relationships. In *Proceedings of IFIP 74*, pages 580–583. North Holland, 1974.
2. J. Biskup. A Formal Approach to Null Values in Database Relations. In J. Minker and J.M. Nicholas, editors, *Advances in Database Theory: Vol. 1*, pages 299–341. Plenum, New York, 1981.
3. Y.L. Breitbart, P.L. Olson, and G.R. Thompson. Database Integration in a Distributed Heterogeneous Database System. In *Proceedings of the International Conference on Data Engineering*, pages 301–310, Washington, DC, February 1986. IEEE Computer Society.
4. E.F. Codd. Missing Information (Applicable and Inapplicable) in Relational Databases. *SIGMOD RECORD*, 15(4):53–78, 1986.
5. E.F. Codd. Extending the Database Relational Model to Capture More Meaning. *ACM Trans. on Database Systems*, 4(4):394–434, December 1979.
6. E.F. Codd. A relational model of data for large shared data banks. *Comm. ACM*, 13(6):377–387, June 1970.
7. C.J. Date. Null Values in Data Base Management, 1982. (Also found in C.J.Date, Relational Database: Selected Writings, 1986, Addison Wesley).
8. C.J. Date. *An Introduction to Database Systems*. Addison-Wesley, Reading, Mass., 1986.
9. T.R. Davies and S.J. Russell. A Logical Approach to Reasoning by Analogy. In *Proceedings of the 10th IJCAI*, pages 264–270, 1987.
10. L.G. DeMichiel. Resolving Database Incompatibility: An Approach to Performing Relational Operations over Mismatched Domains. *IEEE Transactions on Knowledge and Data Engineering*, 1(4):485–493, 1989.
11. R. Fagin. Multivalued Dependencies and a New Form for Relational Databases. *ACM Trans. on Database Systems*, 2(3), September 1977.

12. G. Grahne. Dependency Satisfaction in Databases with Incomplete Information. In *Proceedings of VLDB 84*, pages 37–45. Morgan Kaufmann, 1984.

13. J. Grant. Null Values in a Relational Database. *Information Processing Letters*, 6(5), October 1977.

14. T. Imielinski and W. Lipski. Incomplete Information in Relational Databases. *J.ACM*, 31(4):761–791, October 1984.

15. W. Lipski. On Databases with Incomplete Information. *J.ACM*, 28(1):41–70, January 1981.

16. R.S. Michalski, J.G. Carbonell, and T.M. Mitchell, editors. *Machine Learning: An AI Approach*. Morgan Kaufmann Publishers, 1983.

17. J. Minker and J. Grant. Answering queries in indefinite databases and the null value problem. In P. Kanellakis, editor, *Advances in Computing Research*, pages 247–267. 1986.

18. A. Motro. Extending the Relational Database Model to Support Goal Queries. In L. Kerschberg, editor, *Expert Database Systems*, pages 129–150. Benjamin Cummings, 1987.

19. A. Rajasekar. Inductive Dependencies. Technical Report 189-91, University of Kentucky, Lexington, Kentucky, July, 1991.

20. U.Dayal and H.Y. Hwang. View Definition and Generalization for Database Integration in MULTIBASE. In *Proceedings of Berkley Workshop on Distributed Data Management and Computer Networks*, 1982.

21. J.D. Ullman, editor. *Principles of Database and Knowledge-Base Systems*. Computer Science Press, Rockville, Maryland, 1988.

22. Y. Vassiliou. Functional Dependencies and Incomplete Information. In *Proceedings of VLDB 80*, pages 260–269, 1980.

23. R.L. Winkler and W.L. Hays, editors. *Statistics: Probability, Inference and Decision*. Holt, Rinehart and Winston, New York, New York, 1975.

24. L.A. Zadeh. Fuzzy Sets. *Information Control*, 8:338–353, 1965.

Object-Oriented Database Design Methodologies: A Survey

Il-Yeol Song[1] and E.K. Park[2]

[1] College of Information Studies, Drexel University, Philadelphia, PA 19104

[2] Department of Computer Science, US Naval Academy, Annapolis, MD 21402

Abstract. In this paper, we survey the various methods and tools proposed for object-oriented database (OODB) schema design.   An extensive survey of current literature in this area indicates that structural aspects of OODB are modeled separately from their dynamic behaviors. Even though some of them discuss both at the same time, they merely present either a specification language or notation to impose the operations onto the structure.   Hence, we classify methodologies into two categories: first by their structure and behavior modeling; second by the way relationships are handled.   Our survey will help us identify strengths and weaknesses of individual methodologies, as well as general guidelines for future improvements and extension of methods and tools.   We summarize research issues for OODB schema design.

Keywords: Survey, Object-oriented databases, Database schema, Database design, Methodologies, Tools

1 Introduction

1.1 Introduction and Motivation

There has been a lot of research and literature on object-oriented (OO) database systems in recent years.   OO database systems have a wide acceptance as the next generation DBMS due to the following two main reasons (Atkinson et al. 1989; Kim 1990a; Cattell 1991a; Cattell 1991b; Silberschatz et al. 1990):

(a) They can model new complex applications such as engineering design, office information systems, CASE and multimedia systems, where the variety of semantic relationships among the data cannot be easily captured by existing models.
(b) Through the notions of encapsulation and inheritance, they can reduce the difficulties of developing complex software systems and can enhance the extensibility and reusability of the developed system.

Database design is an iterative process, which includes requirement analysis, conceptual database design, mapping to the physical model, and the physical database design. Database design for OO databases is significantly more complicated than is the design of record-based databases, because OO databases have rich semantics and behavior that must be modeled. Thus, the need for effective design methodologies and tools for OODB is much stronger than that for relational databases (Kim 1990a).

Even though we are not overly interested in the complete definition of design methodology, our notion of a well-defined methodology implies that it should (1) provide a set of guidelines to model and design OODB schema (class and operations) and (2) be easily understood and applicable by application designers with modest database design expertise.

While researchers have developed many database design methodologies for relational database systems, there is no widely accepted methodology for OO database schema design. Widely used approaches to designing relational databases include the entity-relationship approach and its variations (Chen 1976; Teorey et al. 1986; Bruce 1991), NIAM (Nijssen & Halpin 1989), view integration (Batini et al. 1987), as well as more theoretical normalization techniques. OO approaches have been traditionally discussed in the areas of programming languages for problem solving and of artificial intelligence as a method of knowledge representation. Researchers in AI mainly concentrated on the expressive power of the knowledge representation language based on the notion of a frame. As the OO approach is evolving into OO database systems, we need more systematic methodologies to design database schema and to facilitate the maintenance of the integrity of OODB.

There is no well-defined theory to guide OODB design such as normalization in relational database design. Design methodology for OODBs is still a black art (Kim 1990a). Existing OO software design methodologies take little or no account of database aspects. We must devise new design methodologies for OODB applications either by generalizing the existing ones or by providing a migration path from the old to the new methodologies.

Currently over a dozen OODB systems are commercially available (GemStone, ONTOS, Versant, ObjectStore, ITASCA, Objectivity/DB, UniSQL, OpenODB, O_2, IDB, POET, Orion/XR, etc.) or ready to be available (SIM, Postgres, Starburst, PROBE, ENCORE, etc.). However, powerful high-quality OODB systems, which do not provide well-defined, easily-understood and usable design methodologies, do not necessarily result in good OODB applications. What is needed is a formal methodology that takes advantage of the rich semantics of object models. Hence, it is critically important to analyze proposed methodologies against desirable requirements and their applicabilities. This will allow us to identify the weaknesses and strengths of individual methodologies and enhance them, and to provide a basis for the development of tools for OODB schema design.

One of the requirements related to OODB is that OODB must subsume relational database systems and be open to other subsystems (Stonebreaker et al. 1990; Kim 1990a). This implies that database design methodologies for relational database systems must also be evolved for OODB design methodologies. We believe that this evolution of methodologies is extremely important since they provide a migration path from the conventional DB systems to OODB systems.

The rest of this paper is organized as follows: In the rest of Section 1, we classify OODB design methodologies, define our reference object model, and show references to other aspects of OODB systems. In Section 2, we discuss various issues of OODB design methodologies. In Section 3, we survey the various approaches as classified in Section 1.2. Section 4 summarizes the research issues in OODB schema design and concludes our paper.

1.2 Classification of Methodologies

In this section, we discuss the classification of OODB design methodologies. We first classify them by structure modeling and behavior modeling; and then by the way they treat the relationships in ER-like models.

An OO database schema consists of a set of inter-related classes, where each class has a set of attributes representing static structural aspects of the class and a set of operations representing behavioral aspects of the class. According to our survey, no single methodology proposed in the literature suggests a well-defined integrated guideline to design both structural and behavioral aspects of OODB systems. Some of them merely discuss a specification language for both or propose a notation or diagram convention to impose operations on the class structure. In other words, static structures are modeled using one method and dynamic behaviors are modeled using another method, even though they can be specified in one specification language or in one diagrammatic notation.

Methodologies can also be classified by their treatment of relationships (or associations) among objects (in the ER sense). Most OO languages and OODB systems represent relationships using a pair of reference attributes and associated inverse attributes (Cattell 1991a). There are an increasing number of approaches which advocate the explicit modeling of relationship for ease of understanding and maintenance purposes. The advantages and disadvantages of these two approaches must also be analyzed.

Hence, we classify proposed methodologies based on two aspects: first structure vs. behavior; second modeling explicit relationships or not. We note that an approach may be classified into more than one category depending on the emphasis. An extensive survey of methodologies indicates that they can be classified into the following groups:

A. Structure vs. Behavior
   A.1 Modeling Structures
      (1) Using semantic data models such as EER or its variations
         (A) EER models (Navathe et al. 1989; Kappel & Schrefl 1988; Ku et al.1991; Nachouki et al. 1991; Gorman & Choobinch 1991; Engels et al. 1992; Song & Godsey 1993)
         (B) ERC+ model (Parent et al. 1989; Tari 1992)
         (C) CERM (Gotthard et al. 1992)
         (D) BROOM (Norrie 1991)
         (E) NIAM (Troyer 1991; Hamon & Crehange 1991)
         (F) Semantic Net (Bouzeghoub & Metais 1990)
         (G) Other Semantic models (Herzig & Gogolia 1992)

      (2) Using language approach (Sernadas & Fiadeiro 1991; Jungclaus et al. 1991; Hartmann et al. 1992)
      (3) Using software development methodologies (Loomis et al. 1987; Ward 1989; Balin 1989, Booch 1991; Coad & Yourdon 1991; Rumbaugh et al. 1991; Martin & Odell 1992)
      (4) Heuristic approach (Rolland et al. 1989; Chen & Lee 1991; Kearney et al. 1992)
      (5) Theoretical Approach (Delcambre & Davis 1989; Kim 1991b, Sernadas & Fiadeiro 1991; Jungclaus et al. 1991; Andonoff et al. 1992)
      (6) View integration or generation approach (Gotthard et al. 1992; Qutaishat et al. 1992; Saake & Jungclaus 1992; Ling et al.1993)
      (7) Conversion from relational database (Kearney et al. 1992)
      (8) Multi-layered approach (Saake 1991)

   A.2 Modeling Behavior
      (1) Petri net approach (Kappel & Schrefl 1988; Sakai 1990; Kappel & Schrefl 1991; Embley et al. 1992)
      (2) Temporal Logic (Jungclaus et al. 1991; Hartmann et al. 1992; Engels et al. 1992)

(3) State transition diagrams (Booch 1991; Rumbaugh et al. 1991; Shlaer & Mellor 1992; Hall and Gupta 1991)

(4) First-order logic approach (Tari 1992)

B. Association (Relationships)

B.1 With explicit association (Loomis et al. 1987; Rumbaugh 1988; Navathe et al. 1989; Ku et al. 1991; Kilian 1991; Hwang & Lee 1990; Saake 1991; Hamon 1991; Navathe et al. 1991; Troyer 1991; Norrie 1991; Coad & Yourdon 1991; Rumbaugh et al. 1991; Kearney et al. 1992; Embley et al. 1992; Shlaer & Mellor 1992; Tari 1992)

B.2 Without association (Delcambre & Davis 1989; Bouzeghoub & Metais 1990; Hartmann 1992; Andonoff et al. 1992; Hughes 1991; Cattell 1991a, Herzig & Gogolla 1992; Song & Godsey 1993).

In this paper, we focus on the structural aspects of methodologies.

The two major objectives of this study are:

(a) To evaluate proposed methodologies for OODB schema design against OODB design criteria and schema integrity. In addition, approaches to handling "relationships" and relationships between structural modeling techniques and behavior modeling will also be analyzed. This will also help us to build a better methodology for requirements engineering for OODB systems, by providing additional insight into *each* OODB schema design methodology studied and its impact on schema evolution and automatic propagation mechanisms.

(b) To develop a framework for a knowledge based system for OODB schema design and evolution, which conforms to schema integrity and automatic propagation mechanisms. This will also allow us to build multi-model (e.g., EER, NIAM) interfaces for OODB systems, which makes the transition from relational model to OODB more smooth. Hence many people who are already familiar with the existing DB design paradigm will be able to apply their knowledge to new OODB systems.

1.3 Object-Oriented Database Models

There are many OO database systems both as research prototypes and at the commercial level (Cattell 1991a; Cattell 1991b). Even though there is a standardization effort (X3/SPARC/DBSSG/OODBTG 1990), there is no single agreed upon OO data model as yet. Core OO concepts discussed in commercial OO database systems or research prototypes include (Elmasri & Navathe 1988; Kim 1990b; Cattell 1991a; Hughes 1991):

Abstraction	Terms	Modeling
• classification/instantiation	class/object	is-a-class-of
• generalization/specialization	class hierarchy	is-a
• aggregation	object composition	is-a-part-of
• association	relationships	is-associated-with
• identification	object identifier	is-identified-by

Because of the lack of standard terminology, we adopt the following terminology below for our discussion purposes. We will call this model the Reference Object Model (ROM). Exposition of the definitions will be necessarily short because of limited space.

An OODB schema consists of a collection of *classes*. Each class has a set of *instances*, which are the objects belonging to that class. Each class is an abstract data type which has a group of *attributes* (called instance variables in some OO systems) and a set of operations defined on them (classification). These attributes describe properties of the instances of a class. Each object has an object identity independent of the values that it contains (identification). Classes form a set of class hierarchies, forming superclass and subclass relationships (generalization). Subclass objects inherit the attributes and operations of superclasses. The class hierarchy becomes a class lattice in the form of directed acyclic graph (DAG) when a class can have more than one parent class (multiple inheritance). It is common practice to refer to a class lattice as a class hierarchy. Attributes in OODB could be simple attributes, collection attributes (set values, lists, arrays), derived attributes (whose value are computed by procedures or methods), class attributes (whose value represent properties of the class or summary values, rather than each individual instance) or *reference attributes* (which point to other object(s)). Simple attributes are atomic attributes which do not have their own components. They do not have their own identity. They are identified by their values. Examples of the simple attributes are integers, numbers, strings, and other simple values. Set-valued attributes are those which have a set of simple values or a set of other reference objects. Examples of class attributes are average number of players or uniform color of a baseball team. Reference attributes are used to represent relationships between objects (association). A reference attribute can represent either a single object or a set of objects. These attributes may be aggregated to form an object, and objects may be aggregated to form composite objects (aggregation).

While there is a need to standardize many of these components, we must not ignore the need for accompanying methodologies, techniques, and tools to support the design and development of applications within an OO system.

1.4 Other Aspects of OODBs

In this section, we provide some references on other aspects of OODBs. For a survey of semantic data models, which lay out the foundation of object-oriented structural modeling, refer to Hull & King (1987) and Peckham & Maryanski (1988). For a recent summary and a collection of recent work on conceptual modeling, refer to Loucopoulos & Zicari (1992). For a general introduction to OODBs, refer to Hughes (1991), Cattell (1991a), Kim (1990b), or Bertino et al. (1991). For a survey of object-oriented query languages, refer to Bertino et al. (1992). For a summary of strengths and weakness of OODBs, refer to Kim (1991a). For architectural issues in OODBs, refer to Kim (1990c). For the research issues of OODBs, refer to Kim (1990a).

2 Issues in OODB Schema Design

The goal of data modeling is to design a better database. Because of the rich semantics, database design for OO databases is significantly complicated. Thus, the need for effective design methodologies and tools for OODB is much stronger than those for relational databases (Kim 1990a).

A key step in the design of OODBs is the derivation of object classes that describe the data objects required by the applications and the specification of interrelationships among them. This activity is referred to as the logical design of an OODB schema. Most applications require a wide variety of changes before converging to an acceptable schema. OODB schemas tend to be modified frequently during the life time of a database and users tend to arrive at a preliminary design through trial and error using the schema change operations. This activity is referred to as *schema evolution*. After the user modifies the class hierarchy, the resulting class hierarchy must also be in a consistent and non-redundant state. In order to enforce this consistency certain schema updates must be propagated. This activity is called *automatic update propagation*.

Database schema design for OODB can be done using the following phases:
1. Identify real-world entities to be included as objects in the database.
2. Create a definition for each class:
    a. attributes or instance variables (static structure).
    b. methods (behavior).
3. Identify generalization and aggregation hierarchies of objects.
4. Verify schema consistency and inconsistency.
5. Refine the total schema.
6. Continue schema evolution and apply the automatic propagation mechanism throughout the lifetime of the database .

However, these steps involve many hidden issues as identified by different researchers (Nguyen & Rieu 1989; Kim 1990a; Wirfs-Brock & Johnson 1990; Chen & Lee 1991), requiring methodologies and tools. Each design methodology or tool should facilitate all or some of the following points for OODB modeling.

1. Where and how do we start and where do we go next?
2. How do we separate a subset of instances of an object class to form a subclass?
3. What should be the derivation specification of a subclass?
4. Should a certain property be modeled as an attribute or as a class?
5. How should we model database constraints?
6. How should we model database behaviors?
7. What rules are necessary to come up with operations, behaviors and events?
8. How do we enforce schema integrity?
9. How do we automatically propagate schema updates?

A workshop on object-oriented modeling at the OOPSLA conference (Holibaugh 1992) identified eight criteria for OO modeling representation techniques. They are:
1. concise
2. easy to create
3. adjustable in scope
4. difficult to mis-use
5. based on a small set of primitives
6. able to define different levels of abstraction
7. expressible enough to model the problem and its solution
8. able to define the whole problem/solution with one technique (uniformity of representation).

Wirfs-Brock and Johnson (1990) discuss the goals of developing a method in OO design as follows.
1. Should use a model that encourages exploration of alternatives early in the design process.
2. Develop simple tools that help a designer to reason about a design. It should be easy to record and modify design decisions.
3. Develop language-independent methods and guidelines.

These are some research questions we have to evaluate against those proposed methodologies for modeling structures and behaviors. Even though some of these criteria depend on the underlying implemented OODB system architecture, conceptual DB design methodologies should facilitate these as much as possible.

3 OODB Design Methodologies

We believe that OODB schema design methodologies are still in their infancy, requiring a lot of research and experimentation. The methodologies discussed in this section may not be exhaustive, but they are most of what we could collect from the recent relevant literature.

3.1. Classification by Structures and Behaviors

3.1.1 Structure Modeling
3.1.1.1 Translation from Semantic Data Models

There are many semantic data models proposed in the literature. For a survey of research-oriented semantic data models, see Hull & King (1987) and Peckham & Maryanski (1988). Among them, the two most widely used semantic data models for relational database design are EER and NIAM models. We believe that translation methodologies from EER to OODB are especially important, because most existing CASE tools support the EER model or its variations (DBMS 1991). Besides EER and NIAM, IDEF1X (Bruce 1991) methodology, which is another variation of EER, could be studied as well. In this section, we survey translation methodologies from various EER-like models to OO models.

(A) Converting EER models to object-oriented schema (Navathe et al. 1989; Kappel & Schrefl 1988; Ku et al.1991; Nachouki et al. 1991; Gorman and Choobinch 1991; Engels et al. 1992; Song & Godsey 1993)
The ER model and its variations are the most popular approach for relational database design (Chen 1976; Teorey et al. 1986; Batini et al 1991). This is mainly because the ER approach is easy to use; has a sufficient set of primitives to represent many real world semantics; it's easy to translate its schema into other data models such as RM, NM, and HM; and it's easy to communicate with an ER diagram among the people involved in database design and development. As such it is natural to consider the ER model as a starting point of designing an OODB schema. By elaborating this methodology for OODB schema design, we will not lose the valuable knowledge many information engineers have obtained from the design of conventional database systems. Hence, we believe that this will be one of the most promising approaches in designing OODB schema.

The representation of relationships is one of the most fundamental ways in which data models differ. As there are several translation techniques in converting an ERD into a relational model structure depending on how relationships are handled, there could be at least two translation paradigms in translating an ERD into an OODB schema. The first approach is to convert each entity and each relationship into one object. Thus, the resulting schema will keep the structure of the original ER model. We will call this approach as the *stable translation*, since the converted schema is stable against changes in relationship types and their cardinality. There are two approaches using this idea (Navathe et al. 1989; Ku et al. 1991), and both are called the OOER model. Another approach is to combine relationships into object classes using a pair of a reference attribute and its inverse attribute. However, the ternary relationship is created as a separate object class. And thus in this approach the original structure of the ER model is not kept in the target OO schema. We call this approach the *mapped translation*. This method is more complex than stable translation, but will result in a more compact OODB schema. This approach is taken by Hughes (1991), Cattell (1991a) and in most commercial OODB systems.

The stable translation method is advantageous since it can be easily converted from the EER diagram and can be easily compared with other model structures such as the relational model or the network model. Also the maintenance of OODB schema in this structure is easier than in other structures because of its explicit relationship representation. However, it does not allow us to take full advantage of OO concepts where composite objects are allowed. It also results in the proliferation of objects as compared with other methodologies for OODB schema design. Whereas the stable translation can still explicitly show the EER's cardinality constraints in the OODB diagram, the mapped translation only implicitly shows the cardinality by single-valued and set-valued attributes, unless otherwise defined by integrity constraints. Another advantage of mapped translation is that it enforces the notion of encapsulation by incorporating all the relevant concepts under one definition. This issue is further discussed in Section 3.2.

We show rules, used in Song & Godsey (1993), for converting an ERD into an OO schema using the mapped translation approach. Note that we assume an ERD can contain derived attributes, composite attributes and multi-valued attributes as in Elmasri and Navathe (1989).

(1) Entity type:
- Each entity type becomes an object class.

(2) Binary relationships (from entity type A to another entity type B)
(* Note that relationships in ERD are represented by a reference attribute and its inverse attribute in the mapped translation. For example, if there is WORK_ON relationship between EMP and DEPT with many to one cardinality, then the EMP object has a reference attribute DEPT and the DEPT object has an inverse attribute EMP as a reference-set attribute (see 2.2 below). These inverse relationships are necessary for the maintenance of relationship integrity and for two ways of accessing related objects. *)
    (2.1) 1:1: Object class A has a reference attribute B, and object class B has a reference attribute A.
    (2.2) 1:N: Object class A has a reference-set attribute B and object class B has a reference attribute A.
    (2.3) M:N: Create a link object class L for the M:N relationship. Add reference attributes A and B within the link object L. The non-key attributes of the relationship then become properties of L. Object class A and object class B each have a reference-set attribute of type L.

(3) "isa" relationship between A isa B:
Declare as super class B in object class A.

(4) Attributes:
    (4.1) Single-valued attributes: They become simple attributes of the object class with atomic data types.
    (4.2) Multi-valued attributes: If the order of values is important, they become list attributes. Otherwise they become set-valued attributes.
    (4.3) Derived attributes: They become derived attributes whose values are computed by operations.

(4.4) Composite attributes: They become reference attributes whose domain is an object class which consists of attributes making up the composite attribute in the ERD.

(4.5) Attribute of 1:1 relationship: The attribute can be an attribute of a more permanent object (e.g., Department is more permanent than manager).

(4.6) Attribute of 1:N relationship: The attribute becomes an attribute of the N-side object.

(4.7) Attribute of M:N relationship: The attribute becomes an attribute of the link object class created in Rule 2.3.

(5) Weak entity type:

Weak entity type becomes a set-valued attribute of the owner object, where the domain of the set-valued attribute is the weak entity type.

(6) Ternary relationship:

Create an object corresponding to the ternary relationship.

(7) Aggregation in ER model:

(a) Create an aggregated object class G from the relationship enclosed in the aggregate.

(b) Add two participating entity types within G as a reference attribute.

(c) Add non-key attribute of the relationship as simple attributes of G.

(d) Each participating entity type has either a reference attribute or reference-set attribute of type G, depending on the cardinality of relationship between them as in Rules (2.1), (2.2), and (2.3).

Song and Godsey used this rule set and developed a system called KERO (Knowledge based system converting Entity-Relationship diagram into an Object-oriented schema) using Prolog.

The above is just one way of converting an ER diagram into an OO schema. In general, the process of converting an ERD into an OO schema, however, is not deterministic. For example, relationships in an ERD can be mapped into either an attribute, an operation, or an object class. Relationships with non-key attributes can become a separate object class. In addition, handling participation constraints, ternary relationships, and other constraints in OO databases are not clearly analyzed yet. Ling, Teo, and Yan (1993) show another way of converting ERD into an OO schema, and their method is discussed in Section 3.1.1.6. Furthermore, none of these approaches discusses behavior modeling or provides a complete mechanism for encapsulation. It is the nature of non-determinism and left-out problems which require more analysis and research in this area.

Other approaches using EER models include Gorman and Choobinch (1991), Nachouki et al. (1991), and Norrie (1991). Gorman and Choobinch propose an OOERM by extending ERD to include methods and message passing structures. However, the diagram becomes very messy, loses intuitiveness, and cannot represent all messages for most real-world applications. Nachouki, et al. discuss how to integrate logical data access from ERD to define the OODB schema.

(B) Using ERC+ model for object-oriented schema (Parent et al. 1989; Tari 1992)

Parent and Spaccapietra (1989) and Tari (1992) use ERC+ model for OODB modeling. The ERC+ (Entity-Relationship Complex plus generalization) is an extended ER model designed to supporting complex objects, object identity, n-ary relationships, explicit roles for each entity, set-valued and complex-valued attributes. The ERC+ model does not allow relationships to be defined on relationships, or entities to be used as attributes of other entities. Parent and Spaccapietra discuss structure modeling using ERC+ model and ERC+ algebra for the complex object composition and manipulation. The ERC+ model is limited as an OO model. In ERC+, not everything is an object; there are semantic differences between entities, attributes, and relationships; dynamic properties are not modeled. Tari (1992) discusses an elegant approach for both structural modeling using ERC+ model and behavior modeling using the first-order logic. Tari proposes an extension of an ER DDL, called Conceptual Definition Language (CDL), to model behavior using first-order logic. The behavioral part of his work is discussed in Section 3.1.2.

(C) CERM (Gotthard et al. 1992)

Gotthard, Lockemann, and Neufeld (1992) uses the Complex Entity-Relationship model (CERM) to model the structural aspects of OODBs. The CERM is an extended ER model supporting generalization, aggregation, and n-ary relationship. In CERM, objects consist of two parts: a descriptive part and a structural part. A Descriptive part is composed of a number of attributes whose domains are simple primitive types. One or more of these attributes should be designated as key attributes for uniqueness among the objects of the same class. The structural part consists of a set of subobjects (i.e., reference attributes in our reference object model), thus allowing aggregation. The CERM supports n-ary relationships and allows relationship attributes. The classes are organized into a class hierarchy for inheritance property. The view integration approach based on this mode is discussed in Section F of this chapter.

(D) BROOM (Norrie 1991)

Norrie(1991) presents the Binary Relational Object-Oriented Model (BROOM) for a specification of an OO model with relations, developed as part of ESPRIT project. The notion of relations is added to provide support for the direct representation of relationships between entities. It supports multiple kinds of collections such as sets, lists, and bags. Generalization hierarchy could have a covering or disjoint constraints in the classification of subclasses. Norri also shows the translation of a BROOM description into a formal Z specification language. The model is said to have a collection algebra called AQL, but the AQL is not discussed in the paper. Behavioral modeling is not discussed in the paper either.

(E) NIAM (Troyer 1991; Hamon & Crehange 1991)

NIAM is a less well-known technique than EER approach, but has more number of semantic constraints than the EER approach. Database schema translation rules between EER model and NIAM are discussed in (Song & Forbes 1991), and translation from NIAM diagram to OODB is discussed in (Troyer 1991) and called OO-NIAM.

Note that NIAM uses different terms from EER: NOLOT in NIAM is similar to an entity type and LOT in NIAM corresponds to an attribute in the EER. NIAM also explicitly represents relationships between NOLOT and LOT.

The main ideas of Troyer's approach can be summarized as follows:
(1) NOLOT becomes an object class.
(2) LOT becomes an attribute (instance variable) of the object class it belongs
    to.

(3) LOT objects are classified into either internal objects or external objects, depending on whether or not they can be accessed by other objects, thus providing encapsulation.

(4) Graphical representation of methods are shown, but not discussed.

(5) OO-NIAM also supports explicit relationship.

(6) All the NIAM constraints are represented as in NIAM diagram.

Other concepts are straightforwardly converted from NIAM. The proposed graphical notation is extremely complex and can easily get messy, not only because of newly introduced diagram constructs such as internal/external objects and methods, but also because of NIAM's inherent representation of the LOT-NOLOT relationship. In fact, the explicit representation of LOT-NOLOT relationships violates the encapsulation of OODB systems, because it hurts the abstraction capability of hiding LOTs. Even though Troyer argues that explicit modeling of relationships is supported, she does not clearly specify how to handle the explicit association between LOT and NOLOT. Representing participation constraints was not discussed.

Hamon and Crehange (1991) also use NIAM for conceptual modeling and convert its structure into an OO schema, and modify it by adding implementation details through successive refinement. However, more specific guidelines, as in Troyer (1991), are not clearly specified. The overall strategy taken in this paper is quite similar to Rumbaugh, et al. (1991), except for the fact that Hamon and Crehange use NIAM instead of OMT (see Section 3.1.1.3 for OMT of Rumbaugh, et al. 1991).

(F) Using semantic network (Bouzeghoub & Metais 1990).
Bouzeghoub and Metais (1990) use the semantic network for the initial conceptual modeling of an OODB schema. The semantic network is enhanced, in addition to generalization, with the notion of atomic aggregation (object with primitive data type), molecular object (object with complex data type) and integrity constraints including domain cardinalities, functional dependencies, keys, intersection and disjunction of classes. These structures and constraints are encoded by the CO_2 language of O_2 OODBMS.

(G) Other Semantic models (Herzig & Gogolia 1992)
Herzig and Gogolia (1992) discuss the conversion of a fictitious conceptual model to an Object-Based model (OBM). The fictitious model includes modeling constructs from EER, Semantic Data Mode (SDM), IFO, and Functional Data Model (FDM). The OBM has the concepts of key, multi-valued, object-valued attributes as well as complex objects, generalization, categorization, and specialization. "Relationships" are not modeled in the OBM. Behavioral modeling is not discussed either.

3.1.1.2 Using Language Approach (Sernadas & Fiadeiro 1991; Jungclaus et al. 1991)
These approaches are more like OO specification languages rather than modeling languages since they focus on the specification of an OO model without providing proper guidelines for modeling. These languages facilitate detection of errors and consistency checking. Sernadas & Fiadeiro (1991) present an OO specification formalism based on proof-theoretic semantics. In this formalism an object is a description. A description denotes a theory consisting of a signature and a set of formulas. The main advantage of the proof-theoretical semantics is to provide a framework for consistency checking and verification.

Jungclaus, Saake, and Hartmann present a language called T_{ROLL} (Textual Representation of an Object Logic Language) which is a formal OO language for a specification of conceptual modeling. The structure and behavior of an object are specified in a construct called a *template*. The template encapsulates user-defined data types, attributes, events, constraints, and derivation. Static integrity constraints are specified by first-order logic and dynamic constraints are specified by temporal logic. The TROLL supports pre-conditions and post-conditions for process specification. Hartmann, Jungclaus, and Saake (1992) discuss the three different types of aggregation in TROLL. They are static aggregation, dynamic aggregation, and disjoint aggregation. The static aggregation is one whose composition is declaratively described in the conceptual model and can be analyzed at compile time. For example, an Employee class can have Department and Office as its components. These components are fixed at compile time, are not changed during runtime, and the Department and the Location attributes can be shared by multiple objects. Dynamic aggregation allows objects which change the composition at run time. A dynamic aggregate object is not defined at the concept level so it is not shown in the conceptual diagram showing the static structure of an OODB schema. An example of a dynamic aggregate object would be the temporary aggregation of Employee object and Project object related by the relationship to another class. Dynamic aggregate objects allow the database the flexibility to change, adapt, and incorporate the unforeseen needs. The disjoint aggregate object is a special type of the static aggregate whose components are not shared among objects. For example, Dependent attribute in Employee class would not be shared among objects. The language does not have any diagrammatic representation, though.

The direct OO modeling approach is most desirable for a long term solution, but the translation approaches discussed in Section 3.1.1.1 are desirable for short and mid-range term solutions since existing relational databases are expected to continually bloom for next few years.

3.1.1.3 Using OO Software Design Methodologies (Loomis et al. 1987; Ward 1989; Balin 1989; Wirfs-Brock et al. 1990; Booch 1991; Coad & Yourdon 1991; Rumbaugh et al. 1991; Martin & Odell 1992)

Existing OO software design methodologies take little or no account of database aspects. Kilian (1991) describes the differences between OO software design and OODB design as follows:

"Data modeling focuses on the identification of entities and their relationships based on their anticipated queries and transactions, producing a structural representation of mini-world. On the other hand, OO software design focuses on the behavior of objects and thus concentrating on what we can compute with data. In the ER approach, identifying relationship is a very important part of analysis and modeling. In OO software, relationships are of secondary importance (except "isa" relationships). Relationships with other objects are typically implemented by operations (behavior)."

Another difference is that OO analysis has a bottom-up flavor since OO programming does not formalize and elaborate object decomposition. This is acceptable or desirable in the programming phase. However, a database analyst needs to operate in a top-down fashion - especially in the early phase.

In their excellent survey of current research in OO design, Wirfs-Brock and Johnson (1990) present the OO software design technique called responsibility-driven design (Wirfs-Brock, Wilkerson, and Wiener 1990) and states that "although it is often useful to inherit from a concrete class, concrete classes are usually not designed to be reusable by inheritance, but as components." This implies that a concrete class is not recommended to have a subclass. This is not desirable for OODB design. For example, class Employee may have a subclass Manager and a subclass Technician.

Hence, in order to use OO software design methodologies for OODB schema design, data modeling constructs which can support top-down modeling must be supported and persistence of database objects must be considered. Besides a graphical interface for schema definition, browsing and management, data modeling constructs must be supported (e.g., EER, IDEF, NIAM, Express, IDEF1X - extensions for objects). These tools should interface to the DBMS through a data dictionary/directory of the DBMS. Recent OO system analysis books discuss top-down OO modeling concepts and notations, and can be used for initial conceptual modeling of database systems (Coad & Yourdon 1991; Rumbaugh et al. 1991; Booch 1991; Shlaer & Mellor 1992; Embley et al. 1992; Martin & Odell 1992). Most of these models use a variation of EER models for object modeling. For a more survey of OO systems analysis and design methods, refer Monarchi & Puhr (1992).

Loomis, Shah, and Rumbaugh (1987) and Rumbaugh et al. (1991) present object modeling techniques (OMT) for conceptual design. We think that this is just another variation of semantic data models which use different graphical notation for generalization, aggregation, and association relationships. Most concepts and notations in OMT have a counterpart in the EER model except aggregation. (OMT has an explicit notation for aggregation). For example, the qualified relationship in OMT is partially similar to the weak entity of ER modeling. The extra concepts discussed in Loomis, Shah, and Rumbaugh (1987, other than typical EER constructs, are representations of methods inside the object class, two forms of method specialization: override and augmentation, and the notion of transitive and intransitive attributes in aggregation. With *override*, the subclass' methods overrides its superclass' methods. With *augmentation*, the subclass' method is executed first and then the superclass' method, if any, is executed. The transitive attributes are those which are propagated down the aggregation hierarchy, and intransitive attributes are those which are applied to the class as a whole but not to its component classes.

3.1.1.4 Heuristic Approach (Rolland et al. 1989; Chen & Lee 1991; Kearney et al. 1992)

We named the approaches taken by Chen & Lee (1991) and Rolland, Cauvet, and Proix (1989) the heuristic approach, because they do not belong to any of our categories and they do not use any particular paradigm. Chen & Lee discuss several heuristic rules for partitioning subclasses. The approach is neither complete nor comprehensive. In order to design a reasonably well-defined OODB, many more heuristics must be further defined. However, these rules can be used together with other methodologies.

Rolland, Cauvet, and Proix (1991) discuss an interesting approach for OODB schema design. The main ideas of their methodology, besides typical OODB concepts, can be summarized as follows:

• Object behavior consists of two concepts: action and event. Actions are elementary DB operations which alter the value of an object. Events are trigger-like operations.
• Their OODB schema, called O* schema, consists of four hierarchies of object types: event hierarchy, action hierarchy, entity hierarchy and domain hierarchy.
• They specify certain requirements for object structuration as follows:
    (1) Any instances of entity type must be identified.
    (2) Every relationship function between an aggregate object A and one of its component object B must be total and simple (atomic).

(3) The relationship between a member object and a set of object must be total and simple.
(4) Each object has a unique structure (aggregate structure or set structure).
(5) Each action object is defined for only one object.
(6) Any event object is defined for only one object.

As briefly shown above, they consider participation constraints, valuation (simple or complex), and permanency (permanent or variable). They propose a set of heuristic structure for object structuring. It will be interesting to compare their suggested heuristics and structures with EER and NIAM methodologies.

Kearney, Bell, and Hickey (1992) discuss a heuristic technique inferring objects from relational database content in a relational database system. They use the notion of informativeness, based on entropy, to analyze the database content. Their method consists of two steps; first extracting entities and relationships from the database content, and then inferring objects from these structure.

3.1.1.5 Theoretical Approach (Delcambre & Davis 1989; Kim 1991b, Sernadas & Fiadeiro 1991; Jungclaus et al. 1991; Andonoff et al. 1992)

Andonoff, Sallaberry, and Zurfluh (1992) take the normalization approach for an OODB schema design. The designer expresses a set of functional and multivalued dependencies which describe the static and dynamic properties of objects. These dependencies are minimized by computing a minimal cover, and the designer identifies nested classes which model complex objects. This is based on the decomposition algorithms in the normal form for nested relations. However, this approach could have all the typical problems of the normalization approach in relational databases, such as lack of application semantics, non-uniqueness of minimal cover, etc.

Kim (1991b) discusses algorithms for schema verification and undesirable property detection problems such as inconsistent schema, cyclic schema, and redundant is-a hierarchy. For the issues of various schema integrity and invariants related to schema evolution, see Baneerjee et al. (1987), Penney et al. (1987), and Nguyen et al. (1989). Delcambre and Davis (1989) also discuss a framework for algorithmic verification of the structural aspects of the schema. They implemented tools called Canonizer, Classifier and Reporter. The Canonizer converts the user's input schema into the canonical form Classifier can work on. The Classifier discovers any new structural relationships and/or inconsistencies from the input schema to be verified. The Reporter receives the schema from Classifer and identifies redundant classes, empty classes, and cycled class definitions. The Reporter provides interaction with the designer so that the designer's intention can be correctly modeled.

There are many other approaches proposing the specification of OO conceptual schema in terms of language constructs, without any diagrammatic aids. For example, Seranadas and Fiadeiro (1991), discussed in Section 3.1.1.2, present a specification of OO conceptual schema based on proof-theoretic semantics, but not a method of deriving an OO schema. These are approaches which directly build an OODB schema without using any other diagrammatic tools. Though these approaches can help the specification and verification of OO schema with integrity constraints, they are not readily understood by the typical designer and they are system-specific requiring the understanding of the underlying theory or language used. If the user knows how to build those schema hierarchies, then it is a powerful method to employ However, for the user who does not know how to built the OODB hierarchy, they will not help much. Hence, these approaches should be examined after building an initial schema.

3.1.1.6 View Integration or Generation Approach (Gotthard et al. 1992; Qutaishat et al. 1992; Saake & Jungclaus 1992; Ling et al.1993)

The problems and issues of view integration targeted for relational database systems are discussed in Batini et al. (1987). Here, we survey view integration approaches where each input schema is represented in OO models (Gotthard et al. 1992; Qutaishat et al. 1992; Saake & Jungclaus 1992) and OO external schema generation for OO applications (Ling et al.1993).

View integration typically consists of three steps: comparison of schemas; conforming of schemas; merging and restructuring. In the step of comparison of schemas, two types of conflicts are detected: naming conflicts and structural conflicts. The naming conflicts include synonyms (two names for the same semantics) and homonyms (the same name for two different semantics). The problem of homonyms is easy to detect, while the problem of synonyms is difficult to detect and subject to the help of a knowledge based tool and/or a human integrator. The structural conflicts include data type conflicts, dependency conflicts, and primary key conflicts. In the steps of conforming of schemas, the above conflicts are resolved. In the last step, two schemas are merged and restructured for completeness, minimality, and understandability (Gotthard et al. 1992).

Gotthard, Lockemann, and Neufeld (1992) discuss an automated view integration methodology based on structural OO model called Complex Entity-Relationship Model (CERM). They use design database for software engineering applications to illustrate the algorithmic specification of integration activities. The central idea is to compute assumption predicates, that express similarities between structures in two schema to be integrated, and then have a human integrator confirm or reject them. The modeling constructs considered include aggregation, generalization, and versioning. They also discuss a schema integration tool, implemented in Prolog, based on their approach. The challenge of automatic view integration is to let a tool detect schema conflicts as much as possible and resolve them without or with a minimum of human intervention. They conclude that a more formal approach is more desirable than the one they used in their prototype.

Qutaishat, Fiddian, and Gray (1992) also discuss view integration in two different situations: when preexisting schemas of separate databases are integrated into a single unified global schema; and when a set of independent user views are integrated into a global schema. They use an extended object modeling technique of Rumbaugh, et. al (1991) for input schema representation. Their focus is the proper handling of association merging during the process of schema integration. Their approach was implemented in Prolog and called schema meta-integration system (SMIS).

Saake and Jungclaus (1992) discuss the representation of external schema using a OO conceptual modeling language called TROLL which is based on the Oblog object model. Their focus is to formally represent dynamic objects, which are evolving over time, and interface objects, which could be different from conceptual object.

Ling, Teo, and Yan (1993) propose a set of mapping rules which can generate an OO external schema from a normal form entity-relationship model. Their mapping rules are very similar to those used in (Cattell 1991a; Hughes 1991; Song & Godsey 1993). As an example, we point out four major differences between approaches taken by (Ling et al. 1993) and (Song & Godsey 1993):

(1) Ling et al. generate views, while Song and Godsey generate a conceptual schema. This implies that the former can generate redundant views depending on the applications and not every attributes and relationships are always included in the generated external schema.

(2) When a relationship contains one or more non-key attribute (one which is not a foreign key in the relationship), Ling et al. generate a tuple-valued attribute (a composite attribute which has more than one sub-component) for the relationship. Song and Godsey treat them differently depending on the cardinality of the relationship. See Rules 4.5, 4.6, and 4.7. for details in Section 3.1.1.1.

(3) When a ternary relationship contains one or more non-key attributes, Ling et al. use a complex transformation rule and generate nested tuple-valued attributes. Song and Godsey simply create a new class for the ternary relationship and the non-key attributes of the ternary relationship become the attribute of the new class.

(4) Ling et al. do not have a rule for aggregation, while Song and Godsey do.

We note that, in these approaches, they don't define new objects by defining views. They define new interfaces to existing objects by defining only attributes and events being of interest for the objects for the purposes of authorization for restricted object manipulation and attribute value retrieval.

3.1.1.7. Converting existing relational structure to OO schema (Kearney et al. 1992)

Most relational databases are not directly designed; instead, some semantic approaches are used to conceive the conceptual structure of the database first, then it is converted into logical relational schema. This is because relational model structure lacks semantics among the relations except for the foreign keys. Direct conversion from relational to OODB, without using any semantics, can only be done using some heuristics at the instance level, but that is an extremely inefficient approach.

Kearney, Bell, and Hickey (1992) discuss a heuristic technique inferring objects from relational database content in a relational database system. This is further discussed in Section 3.1.1.4.

3.1.1.8 Multi-layered approach (Saake 1991)

The multi-layered approach is a method on an OODB architecture. We included it in this classification since one of the layer is about conceptual modeling and the architecture has an impact on the conceptual modeling in terms of consistency between layers. The approach considers both the data structure and the application dynamics. It consists of four layers: from bottom to top, (1) data layer; (2) object layer; (3) evolution and action layers; (4) application layer. The data layer contains a description of static data structures. The object layer describes the database using a semantic data model including classes, their relationships, attributes, and rules satisfying integrity constraints. Relationships defined in this layer include generalization, specialization, and partitioning. The evolution layer describes the temporary process that creates permanent objects which remain after the process terminates. Descriptions of the correct database state transitions or sequences with the use of pre- and post-conditions, or actions are formulated in the action layer. The final application layer collects all the interacting processes containing interaction of interfaces, transactions, software systems, etc. The layered approach reduces the problems of complexity of a very large design by modularizing the thought process and using consistency checking at each layer. This does have some drawbacks because layer specifications can be contradictory. The layer approach is useful but it needs more well-defined guidance for the resolution of conflicts between layers. Saake (1991) does not provide any specific conceptual modeling or behavior modeling formalism in the paper.

3.1.2 Behavior Modeling

In this section, we briefly survey behavior modeling in OODB systems. Note that we do not include discussion on the transaction modeling (e.g., TAXIS) based on semantic models.

Behavior modeling (also called dynamic modeling) is the modeling of objects and how they and their relationships change over time (Rumbaugh et al. 1991). The major behavior modeling concepts are events which represent external stimuli and states which represent values of objects. Proper behavior modeling helps eliminate ambiguity, inconsistency, and incompleteness.

Class design in an OO model eventually includes two components: attributes and operations. Attributes could be relatively easily modeled from object structure modeling. Operations should be derived from either the functional model, which models processes, or the behavior model, which models events and their triggering operations and state changes. Some simple database operations (such as Create, Delete, Read, Update, Insert_Into-A-Set, Delete_From_A_Set valued attribute, etc.) can be easily stated or systematically generated from the system. What is more difficult is application-specific operations. An end user working on an application may discover that they wish to perform operations which were not modeled by the designer of the object classes. Hence, the challenge to the OODB system is to provide a way for them to express these operations which play the role of SQL in RDBMS. Without them, end-users have to be experienced programmers to accommodate an evolving schema.

For a survey and comparison of various techniques for software requirement specification, see Davis (1988). Below we survey OO behavior modeling approaches.

3.1.2.1 Petri net approach (Kappel & Schrefl 1988; Sakai 1990; Kappel & Schrefl 1991)

Kappel & Schrefl (1988) and Kappel & Schrefl(1991) discuss the behavior diagram based on Petri nets. The types of behavior diagrams in Kappel & Schrefl(1991) include a life cycle diagram which depicts for an object its states, activities, and connections; an activity specification diagram which completes interfaces of operations; an activity realization diagram which implements operations; and an activity invocation diagram which sends messages. States correspond to places of Petri nets, activities to transitions. Instances of object types, which reside in states, correspond to tokens in Petri nets. Every instance of an object type is, at any point in time, in one of several states of its object type. To record its current states, every object has a multi-valued property "inStates." Unlike Petri nets, where a transition is automatically fired if every prestate contains a token, an activity in a behavior diagram must be explicitly invoked for an object which is in every prestate of the activity.
However, the proposed diagram is too big for real world problems, and usability of these diagrams is not clear yet. Sakai (1990) also uses the Petri nets for behavior modeling of objects based on the aggregation concept.

Embley et al. (1992) uses state-nets which is the high-level modification of Petri nets to form the basis of modeling state transitions. State nets represent the states and the transitions of object classes. Unlike other models, the transitions in these state -nets can take time to execute and are represented by a time line for each transition. Events may be modeled as objects by grouping several events in the form of object classes.

3.1.2.2 Temporal Logic (Jungclaus et al. 1991; Hartmann et al. 1992; Engels et al. 1992)

Jungclaus, Saake, and Hartmann (1991) and Hartmann, Jungclaus, and Saake (1992) discuss a language called TROLL (Textual Representation of an Object Logic Language) which is a formal OO language for a specification of conceptual modeling. The structure and behavior of an object are specified in a construct called a *template*. The template encapsulates user-defined data types, attributes, events, constraints, and derivation. Static integrity constraints are specified by first-order logic and dynamic constraints are specified by temporal logic. Engels et al. also uses a specification language based on temporal logic to model temporal integrity constraints.

3.1.2.3 State transition diagrams (Booch 1991; Rumbaugh et al. 1991; Shlaer & Mellor 1992; Hall and Gupta 1991)

Most OO analysis approaches uses state transition diagrams for behavior modeling. In these approaches, a state diagram describes the behavior of a single class of objects. As each object has its own attribute values, each object has its own state, the result of the unique sequence of events that it has received. Each object is independent of other objects and proceeds at its own pace. The behavior modeling technique used by Shlaer & Mellor (1992) is to attach finite state machines to each object class. This technique models the life cycle of the object class behavior, using the Moore model of the state transition diagram. The model consists of a set of states, events, transitions, and actions. States are unique within the model and may be one of three types: creation, current, and final. In describing events, four aspects are described: meaning, destination, label, and data. Transitions are represented using either diagram or tables. A most interesting aspect of this technique is the introduction of the notion of the capability to model the abnormal behavior of an object such as error, unusual events, and failures.

Hall and Gupta (1991) discuss two abstraction mechanism, using an augmented transition network, for modeling transitional change of entities: extension and evolution. Extension abstraction models transitions in which an entity experiencing change retains its existing characteristics while acquiring new ones; evolution abstraction models transitions in which an entity loses some existing characteristics while acquiring new ones.

3.1.2.4 Using First-Order Logic (Tari 1992)

In Section 3.1.1.1, we mentioned that Tari (1992) uses ERC+ model for structure modeling and the Conceptual Definition Language (CDL), based on first-order logic, for behavior modeling. Behavior of an object is represented as a closed formula associated with entity and relationship types. Well-formed formulas are defined in terms of path variables, terms, and atomic formulas. A formula is defined by a name and a logic description, called the body. Formulas are associated with entity and relationship types. The CDL provides the means for explicitly describing classes. Each class consists of the type part (attributes) and the rule part (operations). Using CDL, Tari describes how to map from the conceptual schema to the O_2 schema. The concept of access path preserving is introduced as a method of mapping. An access path is a path that allows navigation from a class to other classes and attributes of a schema. In addition to access paths, constraints and behavior may also be directly mapped using the formula derived during the conceptual modeling.

3.2 Classification by Handling Relationships

As mentioned in Section 3.1.1.1 there are two ways of handling relationships when we translate from ER-like model to an object-oriented model. The first approach is to keep relationships as a valid modeling construct in an object-oriented model (we called this a *stable* approach in Section 3.1.1.1) and the second approach is to represent a relationship in an ER-like model as an instance variable (or pointer) in an OO model (we called this a *mapped* approach in Section 3.1.1.1). In the mapped approach, to simulate the bi-directional property of a relationship, a reference attribute and its corresponding inverse attribute is used. The first approach is taken in Loomis et al. (1987), Rumbaugh (1987), Navathe and Pillalamarri (1989), Hwang & Lee (1990), Kilian (1991), Ku, Youn, & Kim (1991), Troyer (1991), Saake (1991), Hamon (1991), Navathe et al. (1991), Norrie (1991), Coad & Yourdon (1991), Rumbaugh et al. (1991), Kearney et al. (1992), Embley et al. (1992), Shlaer & Mellor (1992), Ling et al. (1993), and Tari (1992). The latter approach is taken in Delcambre & Davis (1989), Bouzeghoub and Metais (1990), Cattell (1991a), Hughes (1991), Hartmann, Jungclaus, and Saake (1992), Andonoff et al. (1992), Herzig & Gogolla (1992), Song & Godsey (1993), and most commercial OODB systems. In this section we elaborate on the advantages and disadvantages of these two approaches.

Most commercial OODBMSs do not support explicitly the relationship as a valid modeling construct since they are mainly rooted in OO programming languages where the notion of instance variable or pointer is used to simulate the relationships.

Rumbaugh (1987) and others who prefer the stable approach argue that
(a) "relationship" is a valid real-world modeling concept;
(b) "relationship" can represent cardinality constraints;
(c) "relationship" has been shown to be a useful abstraction mechanism in the design of large systems, facilitating the decomposition into subsystems;
(d) using instance variables for "relationship" does not allow a designer to distinguish between association and aggregation.

They argue that relationships clearly represent real-world semantics and natural occurrences, whereas an instance variable is simply an artificial construct. Using instance variables for relationships hides relationships within an object, thereby the overall structure of an application domain is not explicitly understood. Cardinality constraints do exist in the real world as well, and should be considered carefully when designing a system. The inclusion of such constraints forces designers to more carefully consider their plans before implementation is too far along to allow appropriate repairs to be made.

Schools who prefer the mapped approach argue that
(a) encapsulation would become a problem because of the necessity of information sharing among the classes appearing in a relationship (Rumbaugh (1987) argues that information-hiding is still possible through the use of methods inherent in classes);
(b) without "relationship" there is only one single unit called class for extensibility and reusability. With a relationship as a modeling construct there are two units for the mechanism of extensibility and reusability;
(c) now there are declarative ways of enforcing the referential integrity between a reference attribute and its corresponding inverse attribute.

For example, Versant OODBMS (1992) has a declarative way of enforcing reference attributes and inverse attributes so that the referential integrity of insertion and deletion can be automatically enforced.

The syntax and semantics of *BiLink* and *BiLinkVstr* classes are explained in Fig. 1 below.

```
BiLink<type,attribute>
        // a storage class of a bi-directional link to another object.
        // used to establish a 1:1 or 1:N bi-directional relationship
        // from the one-side
BiLinkVstr<type, attribute>
        // a variable length storage class of multiple bi-directional
        // links to other objects.
        // used to establish a 1:N or M:N bi-directional relationship
        // from the N-side.
```

Figure 1. Syntax and semantics of Bi-directional relationship

Note that the above two classes are Versant-defined classes in the C++ language for persistence of objects. Suppose there is a one-to-many relationship between the EMPLOYEE and DEPARTMENT classes, meaning that one employee works for a department and a department has many employees working for it. Assume also that we want to represent the name, age, and address of each employee and the department name of each department. The declarative way of enforcing a reference attribute and its corresponding inverse attribute after mapped translation in Versant syntax is shown in Fig. 2 below.

```
class Employee: Public PObject
{
public
        Ename    emp_name;
        int              age;
        string          address;
        BiLink<Department,aSetofEmployees> myDept;
};


class Department: Public PObject
{
public
        string          dname;
        BiLinkVstr<Employee, myDept> aSetofEmps;
};
```

Figure 2. Declarative syntax for inverse attribute in Versant

In Employee class, attribute "myDept" is a reference attribute whose type is "Department" and whose inverse attribute is "aSetofEmployees" in "Department" class. In "Department" class, attribute "aSetofEmps" is a set-valued reference attribute whose element type is "Employee", and whose inverse attribute is attribute "myDept" in "Employee" class.

The value of relationship as a valid modeling construct in OO models needs more research and experimentation to analyze the advantages and disadvantages.

4 Discussion and Summary

Our research focuses on advancing methodologies for OO database schema design. While OO database systems themselves have been widely researched and accepted as next generation database systems, there is no well accepted methodology for OODB schema design. To our knowledge, no comparative analysis on this topic has been done yet.

The research issues we discovered from our survey include:

- The advantages and disadvantages of having a relationship as a modeling construct in an OO model
- A methods of deriving operations for database applications. A systematic method of deriving operations from a process model and a behavior model.
- Consistency and completeness checking between an object model and a behavior model
- Usage and properties of aggregation (See Hartmann et al. 1992, for example)
- Characteristics of reusability in OODB design (How is it different from that of software design?)
- Adopting OO system analysis and design methods to OODB design
- Guidelines for deriving and structuring OODB hierarchy. (What is a good OODB hierarchy? Where do we need to place a new class in a hierarchy?)
- Formal specification of OODB schema and its correctness
- Easy-to-use heuristics and diagram notation for the formal methods
- View integration methodologies
- Developing knowledge-based tools to assist design and reason about the design

Our survey indicates that structural aspects of OODB are modeled separately from their dynamic behaviors. Even though some of them discuss both at the same time, they merely present either a specification language or notation to impose the operations onto the structure without a well-defined integration method. Our survey also shows that there are many new proposals that advocate the explicit modeling of relationships as a valid modeling construct in OO models as opposed to the conventional OO models which hide relationships as instance variables. Therefore, we classified proposed OODB design methodologies into two categories: first by their structure and behavior modeling; second by the way they handle relationships.

According to our survey, there are no OODB design methodologies that provide a set of guidelines to model and design OODB schema (class and operations) and that are easily understood and applicable by application designers with modest database design expertise. Most methods we surveyed are too rigid and lack guidelines. Integrating structural modeling and behavior modeling requires, in particular, much more research and experimentation in terms of modeling power, usability, applicability to problem domains, and consistency and completeness checking between those two models. Advantages and disadvantages of having explicit relationship as a modeling construct should be studied and further analyzed.

We think that as a short term solution the translation methodologies from semantic data models are important for the following main reason: Most existing relational database design methodologies are based on the semantic approach. By utilizing existing methodologies, we will not lose the valuable knowledge of many information engineers, obtained throughout the design and use of conventional database systems. So the transition from existing systems to OODB systems can be smooth once a set of guidelines is developed. For the long term, we need to develop direct object modeling approaches, for both structures and behaviors, which can be proven to be useful independent of database application domains. Ideally, the direct approach should be supported by knowledge-based tools which can assist the designer in selecting a set of objects, their properties, their behaviors, and identifying OODB hierarchies.

OODB design methodologies also differ in the way they handle relationships in the target OODB model. A relationship can remain as a separate link object or can be represented as a reference attribute and an inverse attribute if the target system supports it. Many-to-many relationships are clearly the most compelling reason to keep the relationship as a separate link object, because an attribute of a many-to-many relationship does not belong to any of the participating objects. Methodologies which represent the relationship as a reference attribute claim that they can enforce the property of encapsulation which keeps all the relevant properties of the class under one definition. Further analysis of these approaches from the point of view of performance, integrity, understandability, extensibility, and maintainability is necessary.

Based on our initial research result, we have developed an expert system which converts an EER schema into an OODB schema (Song & Godsey 1993) using the rules stated in Section 3.1.1.1. The system can further generate a set of class specifications in DDL syntax of Versant OODBMS. The expert system was implemented in a public domain tool MIKE (Micro Interpreter for Knowledge Engineering) running on top of Prolog in an IBM PC environment.

Acknowledgements

The work of I. Song was partially supported by grant from the 1992 Drexel Research Scholar Award. The authors would like to thank Heather M. Godsey for her careful proofreading of the paper and for her contribution to the KERO project.

References

Andonoff, E., Sallaberry, C. and Zurfluh, G. (1992). "Interactive Design of Object Oriented Databases," in *Proc. of 1992 CAiSE Conf.*, pp. 128-146.

Andleigh, P.K. and Gretzinger, M.R. (1992). *Distributed Object-Oriented Data-Systems Design*, Prentice-Hall.

Atkinson, M., Bancilhon, F., DeWitt, D., Dittrich, K., Maier, D., Zdonik, S. (1989). "The Object-Oriented Database System Manifesto," in *First Int'l Conf. on Deductive and Object-Oriented Databases*, Kim, W., Nicolas, J.-M., and Nishio, S. (Eds.).

Bailin, S.C. (1989). "An Object-Oriented Requirements Specification Method," May 1989, *CACM*, vol. 32, no. 5, pp. 608-623.

Banerjee, J. and Kim, W. (1987). "Semantics and Implementation of Schema Evolution in Object-Oriented Databases," in *Proc. of 1987 ACM SIGMOD Conf.*, pp. 311-322.

Batini, C., Lenzerini, M. & Navathe, S. (1987). "A Comparative Analysis of Methodologies for Database Schema Integration," *ACM Computing Surveys*, 18:4.

Batini, C., Ceri, S. & Navathe, S.B. (1991). *Conceptual Database Design: An Entity-Relationship Approach.* The Benjamin Cummings.

Bertino, E. and Martino, L. (1991). "Object-Oriented Database Management Systems: Concepts and Issues", *Computer*, Vol. 24, No.4, pp. 33-47.

Bertino, E., Negri, M., Pelagatti, G., and Sbattella, L. (1992). "Object-Oriented Query Languages: The Notion and the Issues," *IEEE Tr. on Knowledge and Data Engineering*, Vol. 4, No. 3, June 1992, pp. 223-237.

Blaha, M.R., Premerlani, W.J., & Rumbaugh,J.E. (1988). "Relational Database Design Using an Object-Oriented Methodology," *CACM*, April 1988, Vol. 31, N0. 4, pp. 414-427.

Booch, G. (1991). *Object-Oriented Design with Applications.* The Benjamin Cummings.

Bouzeghoub, M. and Metais, E. (1990). "A Design Tool for Object Oriented Databases," in *Proc. of 1990 CAiSE conf.*, pp. 365-392.

Bruce, T.A. (1991). *Designing Quality Databases with IDEF1X Information Models*, Dorset House Publishing, New York.

Cattell, R.G.G. (1991a). *Object Data Management: Object-Oriented and Extended Relational Database Systems*, Addison-Wesley, Reading, MA.

Cattell, R.G.G. (1991b). "Next Generation Database Systems", *CACM*, Oct. 1991, vol. 34, No. 10, pp.30-33.

Chen, I.A. and Lee, R.-C. (1991). "An Approach to Deriving Object-Hierarchies from Database Schema and Contents," in *Methodologies for Intelligent Systems*, Z.W. Ras & M. Zamankova (Eds.), Springer-Verlag, 1991. pp. 113-121.

Coad, P. and Yourdon, E. (1991). *Object-Oriented Analysis*, Yourdon Press.

Davis, A.M. (1988). "A Comparison of Techniques for the Specification of External System Behavior," *CACM*, Sept. 1988, Vol. 31, No. 9, pp. 1098-1115.

DBMS (1991). "CASE Tool RoundUp," *DBMS*, July 1991, pp. 62-69.

Delcambre, L.M.L. and Davis, K.C. (1989). "Automatic Validation of Object-Oriented Database Structure," in *Proc. of 1989 Conf. on Data Engineering*, pp. 2-9.

Elmasri, R. and Navathe, S.B. (1989). *Fundamentals of Database Systems*, The Benjamin/Cummings.

Embley, D.W., Kuttz, B.D., and Woodfield, S.N. (1992). *Object-Oriented Systems Analysis: A Model-Driven Approach*, Yourdon Press.

Engels, G., Gogolla, M., Hohenstein, U., Hulsmann, K., etc. (1992). "Conceptual Modeling of Database Application Using an Extended ER Model," *Data & Knowledge Engineering*, 9, pp. 157-204.

Gorman, K. and Choobineh, J. (1991). "An Overview of of the Object-Oriented Entity-Relationship Model (OOERM), in *Proc. of the Twenty-Third Annual Hawaii Int'l Conf. on System Sciences*, Hawaii.

Gotthard, W., Lockemann, P.C., and Neufeld, A. (1992). "System-Guided View Integration for Object-Oriented Databases," *IEEE Transaction on Knowledge and Data Engineering*, Vol. 4, No.1, Feb. 1992, pp. 1-22.

Hall, G. and Gupta R. (1991). "Modeling Transition" in *Proc. of 1991 Int'l Conf. on Data Engineering*, pp. 540-549.

Hamon, C. and Crehange M. (1991). "Object Models and Methodology for Object-Oriented Database Design," in *Specification of Database Systems*, D. Harper and M.C. Norrie (Eds.), Springer-Verlag, pp. 135-153.

Hartmann, T., Jungclaus, R. and Saake, G. (1992). "Aggregation in a Behavior Oriented Object Model," in *Proc. of 1992 ECOOP Conf.*, O.L. Madison (Ed.), Springer-Verlag.

Herzig, R. and Gogolla, M. (1992). "Transforming Conceptual Data Models into an Object Model," in *Proc. of 1992 Int'l Conf. on Entity-Relationship Approach*, Lecture Notes in Computer Science 645, Springer-Verlag, pp. 280-298.

Holibaugh, R. (1992). "Object-Oriented Modeling," OOPS Messenger, Vol. 3, No. 4, October 1992, (Addendum to OOPSLA '91 Proceedings) pp. 73-77.

Hughes, J.G. (1991). *Object-Oriented Databases*. Prentice Hall.

Hull, R. and King, R. (1987). "Semantic Database Modeling: Survey, Applications, and Research Issues," *ACM Computing Surveys*, Vol. 19, No. 3, September 1987, pp. 201-260.

Hwang, S. & Lee, S. (1990). "An Object-Oriented Approach for Modeling Relationships and Constraints Based on Abstraction Concept," in *Proc. of 1990 Int'l Conf. on Database and Expert Systems Applications*, Vienna Austria, August 29-31, 1990, pp.30-34.

Jungclaus, R., Saake, G., Hartmann T. (1991). "Language Features for Object-Oriented Conceptual Modeling," in *Proc. of 10th Int'l Conf. on Entity-Relationship Approach*, Sam Mateo, 1991, pp. 309-324.

Kappel, G. & Schrefl, M. (1988) "A Behavior Integrated Entity-Relationship Approach for the Design of Object-Oriented Databases," in*Proc. of 7th Int'l Conf. on Entity-Relationship Approach*, Batini, C. (Ed.), pp.175-192.

Kappel, G. & Schrefl, M. (1991) "Object/Behavior Diagrams," in*Proc. of 7th Int'l Conf. on Data Engineerin*, pp.530-539..

Kearney, S.M., Bell, D.A., and Hickey, R. (1992). "Inferring Abstract Objects in a Database," in *Proc. of First Int'l Conf. on Information and Knowledge Management (CIKM '92)*, Baltimore, MD, pp. 318-325.

Kilian, M.F. (1991). "Bridging the Gap Between O-O and E-R," in *10th Int'l Conf. on Entity-Relationship Approach*, Teorey, T. (Ed.), Nov. 13-15, 1991, San Mateo, CA, pp. 445-458.

Kim, W. (1990a). "Object-Oriented Databases: Definition and Research Directions," *IEEE Transaction on Knowledge and Data Engineering.* 2(3), pp. 327-341.

Kim, W. (1990b). *Introduction to Object-Oriented Databases*, The MIT Press.

Kim, W. (1990c). "Architectural Issues in Object-Oriented Databases," J. of Object-Oriented Programming, vol. 2, no. 6, March/April 1990.

Kim, W. (1991a). "Object-Oriented Database Systems: Strengths and Weaknesses," J. of Object-Oriented Programming, vol. 4, No. 4, July/August 1991.

Kim, H.-J. (1991b). "Algorithmic and Computational Aspects of Object-Oriented Schema Design," in *Object-Oriented Databases with Applications to CASE, Networks, and VLSI CAD*, Gupta, R. & Horowitz, E. (Eds.), Prentice-Hall, pp. 26-61.

Ku, C.S., Youn, C. & Kim, H.-J. (1991). "An Object-Oriented Entity-Relationship Model," 1991 ISMM International Conference on *Computer Applications in Design, Simulation and Analysis*," Las Vegas, Nevada, March 19-21, 1991, PP. 55-58.

Lazimi, R. (1989), "EER Model and Object-Oriented Representation for Data Management, Process Modeling, and Decision Support," in *Proc. of 8th Int'l Conf. on Entity-Relationship Approach*, pp. 136-156.

Ling, T.-W., Teo, P-K., and Yan, L-L. (1993). "Generating Object-Oriented Views from an ER-Based Conceptual Schema," in Proc. of *the 3rd Int'l Symposium on Database Systems for Advanced Applications (DASFAA '93)*, Taejeon, Korea, April 6-8, 1993, pp. 148-155.

Loomis, M.E.S., Shah, A.V., & Rumbaugh, J.E. (1987). "An Object Modeling Technique for Conceptual Design," in *ECOOP '87, European Conference on Object-Oriented Programming*, Paris, France, June 1987, Lecture Notes in Computer Science 267, Springer-Verlag, pp.192-202.

Loucopoulos, P. and Zicari, R. (Eds.) (1992). *Conceptual Modeling, Databases, and CASE*. John Wiley.

Monarchi, D.E. and Puhr, G.I. (1992). "A Research Typology for Object-Oriented Analysis and Design," *CACM*, Vol.35, No.9., Sept. 1992, pp.35-46.

Mannino, M.V. and Choi, I.J. (1991). "Tutorial on Object-Oriented Modleing and Reasoning (Extended Abstract)," in *Entity-Relationship Approach: The Core of Conceptual Modeling*, H. Kangassalo (Ed.), North-Holland, pp. 487-496.

Martin, J. and Odell, J., *Object-Oriented Analysis and Design*, Prentice Hall, Englewood Cliffs, N.J., 1992.

Monarchi, D.E. and Puhr, G.I. (1992). "A Research Typology for Object-Oriented Analysis and Design," CACM, Vol.35, No.9., Sept. 1992, pp.35-46.

Nachouki, J., Chastang, M.P. and Briand, H. (1991). "From Entity-Relationship Diagram to An Object Oriented Database," in *Proc. of 10th Int'l Conf. on Entity-Relationship Approach*, pp. 459-481.

Navathe, S.B. & Pillalamarri (1989). "OOER: Toward Making the E-R Approach Object-Oriented," in *Proc. of 8th Int'l Conf. on Entity-Relationship Approach*, pp.55-76.

Navathe, S.B., Geum, S., Desai, D.K., and Lam, H. (1990). "Conceptual Design for Non-Database Experts with an Interactive Schema Tailoring Tool," in *Proc. of 9th Int'l Conf. on Entity-Relationship Approach*, Swiss.

Nguyen, G.T & Rieu, D. (1989). "Schema Evolution in Object-Oriented Database Systems," *Data & Knowledge Engineering* 4(1989), pp. 43-67.

Nijssen, G. M. and Halpin, T. A. (1989). *Conceptual Schema and Relational Database Design: A Fact Oriented Approach*, Prentice Hall of Australia.

Norrie, M.C. (1991). "A Specification of an Object-Oriented Data Model with Relations," in *Specification of Database Systems*, D.J. Harper and M.C. Norrie (Eds.), Springer-Verlag.

Parent, C. and Spaccapietra, S. (1989). "About Entities, Complex Objects and Object-oriented Data Models," in *Information System Concepts: An In-depth Analysis*, E.D. Falkenberg and P. Lindgreen (Eds.), Noth-Holland, pp. 193-223.

Peckham, J. and Maryanski, F. (1988). "Semantic Data Models," *ACM Computing Surveys*, Vol.20, No.3, September 1988, pp. 153-189.

Penny, D.J. and Stein, J. (1987). "Class Modification in the GemStone Object-Oriented DBMS," in *Proc. of 1987 OOPSLA*, pp. 111-117.

Qutaishat, M.A., Fiddian, N.J., Gray, W.A. (1992). "Association Merging in a Schema Meta-Integration System for a Heterogeneous Object-Oriented Database Environment," in *Advanced Database Systems*, BNCOD 10, P.M.D. Gray and R.J. Lucas (Eds.), Lecture Notes in Computer Science 618, Springer-Verlag, pp. 210-226.

Rolland, C., Cauvet, C, & Proix, C. (1989). "Methodology and Tool for Object-Oriented Database Design," in the *Proc. of 7th British National Conf. on Databases (BNCOD 7)*, Williams, M.H. (Ed.) July 1989.

Rumbaugh, J. (1987). "Relations as Semantic Constructs in an Object-Oriented Language" in *Proc. of the ACM Conf. on OOPSLA*, Orlando, Florida, October 1987.

Rumbaugh, J. (1988). "Controlling Propagation of Operations using Attributes on Relations," in *Proc. of the ACM Conf. on OOPSLA*, San Diego, CA, September 1988.

Rumbaugh, J. , Blaha, M., Premerlani, W., Eddy, F., and Lorensen, W. (1991). *Object-Oriented Modeling and Design*, Prentice-Hall.

Saake, G. (1991). "Conceptual Modeling of Database Applications," in *Information Systems and Artificial Intelligence: Integrating Aspects*, D. Karagiannis (Ed.), Lecture Notes in Computer Science 474, Springer-Verlag, pp.214-232.

Saake, G. and Jungclaus, R. (1992). "Views and Formal Implementation in a Three-Level Schema Architecture for Dynamic Objects," in *Advanced Database Systems*, BNCOD 10, P.M.D. Gray and R.J. Lucas (Eds.), Lecture Notes in Computer Science 618, Springer-Verlag, pp. 78-95.

Sakai, H. (1990). "An Object Behavior Modeling Method," in the Proc. of *1990 Int;l Conf. on Database and Expert Systems Applications*," Vienna, Austria, August, August 29-31, 1990, pp.42-48.

Schrefl, M. & Kappel, G. (1991). "Cooperation Contracts," in *Proc. of 10th Int'l Conf. on Entity-Relationship Approach*, Teorey, T. (Ed.), San Mateo, Oct. 23-25, 1991, pp. 285-307.

Sernadas, C. & Fiadeiro, J. (1991). "Towards Object-Oriented Conceptual Modeling," *Data & Knowledge Engineering* vol. 6, pp. 479-508.

Shlaer, S. and Mellor, S.J. (1992). *Object Lifecycles Modeling the World in States*, Yourdon Press.

Silberschatz, A., Stonebraker, M., and Ullman, J. (1990). "Database Systems: Achievements and Opportunities," *ACM SIGMOD Record*, 19(4). December 1990, pp.6-22.

Song, I.-Y. and Forbes, E. (1991). "Schema Conversion Rules between EER and NIAM Models," in *10th Int'l Conf. on Entity-Relationship Approach*, Teorey, T. (Ed.), Oct. 23-25, 1991, San Mateo, CA, pp. 417-444.

Song, I.-Y. and Godsey, H.M. (1993) "A Knowledge Based System Converting ER Model into an Object-Oriented Database Schema," in Proc. of *the 3rd Int'l Symposium on Database Systems for Advanced Applications (DASFAA '93)*, Taejeon, Korea, April 6-8, 1993, pp. 287-294.

Stonebraker, M., Rowe, L.A., etc. (1990). Third-Generation Database System Manifesto," *SIGMOD Record*, 19(3), pp.31-44.

Tari, Z. (1992). "On the Design of Object-Oriented Databases," in *Proc. of 1992 Int'l Conf. on Entity-Relationship Approach*, Lecture Notes in Computer Science 645, Springer-Verlag, pp. 388-405.

Teorey, T.J. (1990). *Database Modeling and Design: The Entity-Relationship Approach*. Morgan Kauffman Publishers, Inc.

Teorey, T.J., Yang, D., and Fry, J.P. (1986). "A Logical Design Methodology for Relational Databases Using the Extended Entity-Relationship Model," *ACM Computing Surveys*, 18:12, June, pp. 197-222.

Troyer, O.De (1991). "The OO-Binary Relationship Model: A Truly Object-Oriented Conceptual Model," in *Advanced Information Engineering*, Lecture Notes in Computer Science 489, Andersen, R., Bubenko jr., J.A. & Solverg, A. (Eds.), pp. 561-578.

Versant (1992). *Versant ODBMS, C++/Versant*, Versant Object Technology.

Ward, P.T. (1989). "How to Integrate Object-Orientation with Structured Analysis and Design," *IEEE Software*, March 1989, pp. 75-82.

Wirfs-Brock, R.J. and Johnson, R.E. (1990). "Surveying Current Research in Object-Oriented Design," *CACM*, Vol.33, No.9, September 1990, pp.104-124.

Wirfs-Brock, R., Wilkinson, B. and Wiener, L. (1990). *Designing Object-Oriented Software.* Prentice Hall.

X3/SPARC/DBSSG/OODBTG (1990). *Preliminary Proceedings of the First OODB Standardization Workshop*, Atlantic City, NJ, May 22, 1990.

Lecture Notes in Computer Science

For information about Vols. 1–675
please contact your bookseller or Springer-Verlag

Vol. 676: Th. H. Reiss, Recognizing Planar Objects Using Invariant Image Features. X, 180 pages. 1993.

Vol. 677: H. Abdulrab, J.-P. Pécuchet (Eds.), Word Equations and Related Topics. Proceedings, 1991. VII, 214 pages. 1993.

Vol. 678: F. Meyer auf der Heide, B. Monien, A. L. Rosenberg (Eds.), Parallel Architectures and Their Efficient Use. Proceedings, 1992. XII, 227 pages. 1993.

Vol. 679: C. Fermüller, A. Leitsch, T. Tammet, N. Zamov, Resolution Methods for the Decision Problem. VIII, 205 pages. 1993. (Subseries LNAI).

Vol. 680: B. Hoffmann, B. Krieg-Brückner (Eds.), Program Development by Specification and Transformation. XV, 623 pages. 1993.

Vol. 681: H. Wansing, The Logic of Information Structures. IX, 163 pages. 1993. (Subseries LNAI).

Vol. 682: B. Bouchon-Meunier, L. Valverde, R. R. Yager (Eds.), IPMU '92 – Advanced Methods in Artificial Intelligence. Proceedings, 1992. IX, 367 pages. 1993.

Vol. 683: G.J. Milne, L. Pierre (Eds.), Correct Hardware Design and Verification Methods. Proceedings, 1993. VIII, 270 Pages. 1993.

Vol. 684: A. Apostolico, M. Crochemore, Z. Galil, U. Manber (Eds.), Combinatorial Pattern Matching. Proceedings, 1993. VIII, 265 pages. 1993.

Vol. 685: C. Rolland, F. Bodart, C. Cauvet (Eds.), Advanced Information Systems Engineering. Proceedings, 1993. XI, 650 pages. 1993.

Vol. 686: J. Mira, J. Cabestany, A. Prieto (Eds.), New Trends in Neural Computation. Proceedings, 1993. XVII, 746 pages. 1993.

Vol. 687: H. H. Barrett, A. F. Gmitro (Eds.), Information Processing in Medical Imaging. Proceedings, 1993. XVI, 567 pages. 1993.

Vol. 688: M. Gauthier (Ed.), Ada-Europe '93. Proceedings, 1993. VIII, 353 pages. 1993.

Vol. 689: J. Komorowski, Z. W. Ras (Eds.), Methodologies for Intelligent Systems. Proceedings, 1993. XI, 653 pages. 1993. (Subseries LNAI).

Vol. 690: C. Kirchner (Ed.), Rewriting Techniques and Applications. Proceedings, 1993. XI, 488 pages. 1993.

Vol. 691: M. Ajmone Marsan (Ed.), Application and Theory of Petri Nets 1993. Proceedings, 1993. IX, 591 pages. 1993.

Vol. 692: D. Abel, B.C. Ooi (Eds.), Advances in Spatial Databases. Proceedings, 1993. XIII, 529 pages. 1993.

Vol. 693: P. E. Lauer (Ed.), Functional Programming, Concurrency, Simulation and Automated Reasoning. Proceedings, 1991/1992. XI, 398 pages. 1993.

Vol. 694: A. Bode, M. Reeve, G. Wolf (Eds.), PARLE '93. Parallel Architectures and Languages Europe. Proceedings, 1993. XVII, 770 pages. 1993.

Vol. 695: E. P. Klement, W. Slany (Eds.), Fuzzy Logic in Artificial Intelligence. Proceedings, 1993. VIII, 192 pages. 1993. (Subseries LNAI).

Vol. 696: M. Worboys, A. F. Grundy (Eds.), Advances in Databases. Proceedings, 1993. X, 276 pages. 1993.

Vol. 697: C. Courcoubetis (Ed.), Computer Aided Verification. Proceedings, 1993. IX, 504 pages. 1993.

Vol. 698: A. Voronkov (Ed.), Logic Programming and Automated Reasoning. Proceedings, 1993. XIII, 386 pages. 1993. (Subseries LNAI).

Vol. 699: G. W. Mineau, B. Moulin, J. F. Sowa (Eds.), Conceptual Graphs for Knowledge Representation. Proceedings, 1993. IX, 451 pages. 1993. (Subseries LNAI).

Vol. 700: A. Lingas, R. Karlsson, S. Carlsson (Eds.), Automata, Languages and Programming. Proceedings, 1993. XII, 697 pages. 1993.

Vol. 701: P. Atzeni (Ed.), LOGIDATA+: Deductive Databases with Complex Objects. VIII, 273 pages. 1993.

Vol. 702: E. Börger, G. Jäger, H. Kleine Büning, S. Martini, M. M. Richter (Eds.), Computer Science Logic. Proceedings, 1992. VIII, 439 pages. 1993.

Vol. 703: M. de Berg, Ray Shooting, Depth Orders and Hidden Surface Removal. X, 201 pages. 1993.

Vol. 704: F. N. Paulisch, The Design of an Extendible Graph Editor. XV, 184 pages. 1993.

Vol. 705: H. Grünbacher, R. W. Hartenstein (Eds.), Field-Programmable Gate Arrays. Proceedings, 1992. VIII, 218 pages. 1993.

Vol. 706: H. D. Rombach, V. R. Basili, R. W. Selby (Eds.), Experimental Software Engineering Issues. Proceedings, 1992. XVIII, 261 pages. 1993.

Vol. 707: O. M. Nierstrasz (Ed.), ECOOP '93 – Object-Oriented Programming. Proceedings, 1993. XI, 531 pages. 1993.

Vol. 708: C. Laugier (Ed.), Geometric Reasoning for Perception and Action. Proceedings, 1991. VIII, 281 pages. 1993.

Vol. 709: F. Dehne, J.-R. Sack, N. Santoro, S. Whitesides (Eds.), Algorithms and Data Structures. Proceedings, 1993. XII, 634 pages. 1993.

Vol. 710: Z. Ésik (Ed.), Fundamentals of Computation Theory. Proceedings, 1993. IX, 471 pages. 1993.

Vol. 711: A. M. Borzyszkowski, S. Sokołowski (Eds.), Mathematical Foundations of Computer Science 1993. Proceedings, 1993. XIII, 782 pages. 1993.

Vol. 712: P. V. Rangan (Ed.), Network and Operating System Support for Digital Audio and Video. Proceedings, 1992. X, 416 pages. 1993.

Vol. 713: G. Gottlob, A. Leitsch, D. Mundici (Eds.), Computational Logic and Proof Theory. Proceedings, 1993. XI, 348 pages. 1993.

Vol. 714: M. Bruynooghe, J. Penjam (Eds.), Programming Language Implementation and Logic Programming. Proceedings, 1993. XI, 421 pages. 1993.

Vol. 715: E. Best (Ed.), CONCUR'93. Proceedings, 1993. IX, 541 pages. 1993.

Vol. 716: A. U. Frank, I. Campari (Eds.), Spatial Information Theory. Proceedings, 1993. XI, 478 pages. 1993.

Vol. 717: I. Sommerville, M. Paul (Eds.), Software Engineering – ESEC '93. Proceedings, 1993. XII, 516 pages. 1993.

Vol. 718: J. Seberry, Y. Zheng (Eds.), Advances in Cryptology – AUSCRYPT '92. Proceedings, 1992. XIII, 543 pages. 1993.

Vol. 719: D. Chetverikov, W.G. Kropatsch (Eds.), Computer Analysis of Images and Patterns. Proceedings, 1993. XVI, 857 pages. 1993.

Vol. 720: V.Mařík, J. Lažanský, R.R. Wagner (Eds.), Database and Expert Systems Applications. Proceedings, 1993. XV, 768 pages. 1993.

Vol. 721: J. Fitch (Ed.), Design and Implementation of Symbolic Computation Systems. Proceedings, 1992. VIII, 215 pages. 1993.

Vol. 722: A. Miola (Ed.), Design and Implementation of Symbolic Computation Systems. Proceedings, 1993. XII, 384 pages. 1993.

Vol. 723: N. Aussenac, G. Boy, B. Gaines, M. Linster, J.-G. Ganascia, Y. Kodratoff (Eds.), Knowledge Acquisition for Knowledge-Based Systems. Proceedings, 1993. XIII, 446 pages. 1993. (Subseries LNAI).

Vol. 724: P. Cousot, M. Falaschi, G. Filè, A. Rauzy (Eds.), Static Analysis. Proceedings, 1993. IX, 283 pages. 1993.

Vol. 725: A. Schiper (Ed.), Distributed Algorithms. Proceedings, 1993. VIII, 325 pages. 1993.

Vol. 726: T. Lengauer (Ed.), Algorithms – ESA '93. Proceedings, 1993. IX, 419 pages. 1993

Vol. 727: M. Filgueiras, L. Damas (Eds.), Progress in Artificial Intelligence. Proceedings, 1993. X, 362 pages. 1993. (Subseries LNAI).

Vol. 728: P. Torasso (Ed.), Advances in Artificial Intelligence. Proceedings, 1993. XI, 336 pages. 1993. (Subseries LNAI).

Vol. 729: L. Donatiello, R. Nelson (Eds.), Performance Evaluation of Computer and Communication Systems. Proceedings, 1993. VIII, 675 pages. 1993.

Vol. 730: D. B. Lomet (Ed.), Foundations of Data Organization and Algorithms. Proceedings, 1993. XII, 412 pages. 1993.

Vol. 731: A. Schill (Ed.), DCE – The OSF Distributed Computing Environment. Proceedings, 1993. VIII, 285 pages. 1993.

Vol. 732: A. Bode, M. Dal Cin (Eds.), Parallel Computer Architectures. IX, 311 pages. 1993.

Vol. 733: Th. Grechenig, M. Tscheligi (Eds.), Human Computer Interaction. Proceedings, 1993. XIV, 450 pages. 1993.

Vol. 734: J. Volkert (Ed.), Parallel Computation. Proceedings, 1993. VIII, 248 pages. 1993.

Vol. 735: D. Bjørner, M. Broy, I. V. Pottosin (Eds.), Formal Methods in Programming and Their Applications. Proceedings, 1993. IX, 434 pages. 1993.

Vol. 736: R. L. Grossman, A. Nerode, A. P. Ravn, H. Rischel (Eds.), Hybrid Systems. VIII, 474 pages. 1993.

Vol. 737: J. Calmet, J. A. Campbell (Eds.), Artificial Intelligence and Symbolic Mathematical Computing. Proceedings, 1992. VIII, 305 pages. 1993.

Vol. 738: M. Weber, M. Simons, Ch. Lafontaine, The Generic Development Language Deva. XI, 246 pages. 1993.

Vol. 739: H. Imai, R. L. Rivest, T. Matsumoto (Eds.), Advances in Cryptology – ASIACRYPT '91. X, 499 pages. 1993.

Vol. 740: E. F. Brickell (Ed.), Advances in Cryptology – CRYPTO '92. Proceedings, 1992. X, 593 pages. 1993.

Vol. 741: B. Preneel, R. Govaerts, J. Vandewalle (Eds.), Computer Security and Industrial Cryptography. Proceedings, 1991. VIII, 275 pages. 1993.

Vol. 742: S. Nishio, A. Yonezawa (Eds.), Object Technologies for Advanced Software. Proceedings, 1993. X, 543 pages. 1993.

Vol. 743: S. Doshita, K. Furukawa, K. P. Jantke, T. Nishida (Eds.), Algorithmic Learning Theory. Proceedings, 1992. X, 260 pages. 1993. (Subseries LNAI)

Vol. 744: K. P. Jantke, T. Yokomori, S. Kobayashi, E. Tomita (Eds.), Algorithmic Learning Theory. Proceedings, 1993. XI, 423 pages. 1993. (Subseries LNAI)

Vol. 745: V. Roberto (Ed.), Intelligent Perceptual Systems. VIII, 378 pages. 1993. (Subseries LNAI)

Vol. 746: A. S. Tanguiane, Artificial Perception and Music Recognition. XV, 210 pages. 1993. (Subseries LNAI)

Vol. 747: M. Clarke, R. Kruse, S. Moral (Eds.), Symbolic and Quantitative Approaches to Reasoning and Uncertainty. Proceedings, 1993. X, 390 pages. 1993.

Vol. 748: R. H. Halstead Jr., T. Ito (Eds.), Parallel Symbolic Computing: Languages, Systems, and Applications. Proceedings, 1992. X, 419 pages. 1993.

Vol. 749: P. A. Fritzson (Ed.), Automated and Algorithmic Debugging. Proceedings, 1993. VIII, 369 pages. 1993.

Vol. 750: J. L. Diaz-Herrera (Ed.), Software Engineering Education. Proceedings, 1994. XII, 601 pages. 1994.

Vol. 751: B. Jähne, Spatio-Temporal Image Processing. XII, 208 pages. 1993.

Vol. 752: T. W. Finin, C. K. Nicholas, Y. Yesha (Eds.), Information and Knowledge Management. Proceedings, 1992. VII, 142 pages. 1993.

Vol. 753: L. J. Bass, J. Gornostaev, C. Unger (Eds.), Human-Computer Interaction. Proceedings, 1993. X, 388 pages. 1993.